LIVING THROUGH MIDDLE AGE

a Consumer Publication

**LIVING
THROUGH
MIDDLE AGE**

Consumers' Association
publishers of **Which?**
14 Buckingham Street
London WC2N 6DS

a Consumer Publication

edited by   Edith Rudinger

published by   Consumers' Association
publishers of **Which?**

Consumer Publications are
available from Consumers'
Association and from booksellers. Titles of other Consumer
Publications are given at the
end of this book.

© Consumers' Association March 1976
reprinted May 1976
revised reprint September 1978
ISBN 0 85202 154 2

 Computer typeset
and printed offset litho
by Page Bros (Norwich) Ltd

CONTENTS

Living through middle age   *page* 1
Normal physical changes   3
  eyes   3
  teeth   6
  hair   10
  skin   18
  feet   25
Aspects of health   28
  weight   28
  calories and food   35
  exercise   46
  sleeping   48
  alcohol   50
  smoking   54
Diseases common in middle age 57
  circulatory disorders   58
  respiratory disorders   65
  digestive disorders   67
  diabetes   70
The menopause   72
  sex and fertility   74
  hot flushes   77
  the change   79
  treatment   85
  gynaecological treatment   89
Elderly dependants   99
Psychological aspects   102
  depression   106
  sex and impotence   107
Index   114

If you ask people when middle age begins, a young person will say at 30, an older person will say at 55. Let us say it begins after 40 and goes on until about 60. These are the years during which a person's fitness is important not only to survive, but also to provide sufficient energy to cope with the responsibilities. It is a very full period of life, in which many ambitions will be fulfilled so far as career is concerned. Most middle-aged people have important family responsibilities, with the care of husband or wife and children, and perhaps elderly parents needing support. It is a time when many claims are made on you—ageing relatives, friends' crises, demands of teenagers—and you may have to reassess your priorities so as not to get overwhelmed and exhaust your resources, both mental and physical. You may have to modify what you do or the way you do it, but it is important not to stop doing what you enjoy and are good at so as to retain self-respect, a zest for life and an ability to adapt to change whatever it may need to be. When the financial and emotional problems of a growing family have eased, there is greater freedom to develop new interests and activities. It is particularly important at this age to retain flexibility of mind as well as body, and to make a conscious effort to remain open to the stimulus of new ideas and different people.

Normal physical changes with age

The physical changes people can normally expect depend to some extent on their constitution as inherited from their parents. Whether or not a man has kept his hair, for instance, depends mainly on his genetic endowment; men can roughly be divided into those who come from families who keep their hair, and those who do not.

The eyes

A normal change that occurs in the eye with age is presbyopia. By the age of about 48, most people with normal sight will notice that it has become impossible to read small print at the usual reading distance of 10 to 12 inches, and that it is becoming necessary to hold the book farther and farther away, especially in a poor light. This happens because the lens within the eye has become less flexible and can no longer be shaped (by the ciliary muscle) to focus on to the retina small shapes such as print—or the eye of a needle. Wearing glasses with a weak magnifying lens will rectify this.

Glasses will have to be worn for reading and, because the sight continues to change, the eyes should be checked annually for a few years so that new glasses can be prescribed if necessary. Eyes can be tested under the national health service without charge.

The onset of presbyopia is delayed in a slightly short-sighted person. People who wear glasses because of short-sightedness start taking off their glasses for close work. Long-sighted people for whom the onset of presbyopia is earlier, usually need new glasses for reading only which would be too strong for distant vision. When eventually two pairs of glasses would be needed—

one for distance only, the other for reading—the alternative is to have bifocals.

Bifocal glasses consist of two lenses incorporated in one set of spectacles: the upper part to correct distance vision, with a small lower segment for close vision. It takes a little while to get accustomed to bifocals. When looking down—at stairs, for instance—it helps to move the whole head rather than just the eyes.

Difficulty in reading leads to tension and may cause or aggravate headache. There is no such thing as eyestrain in the sense of damaging the eyes by straining to read when vanity refuses spectacles. Nor does wearing glasses regularly make the eyes lazy or dependent. There is a common but mistaken belief that wearing the wrong glasses, or not wearing those that have been prescribed, will cause damage to the eyes. Fortunately, this is not so, and all that happens in these circumstances is that you cannot see very well.

The amount of light required for comfortable close work when aged 50 is twice that at 25 years of age, due to normal changes in the eye. Increasing the lamp wattage or bringing the light nearer improves vision and visual comfort. It is normal for the eyes to adapt less well to darkness and to have an increased intolerance to headlamp glare. Yellow-tinted night driving glasses may create the illusion of improving visual quality and comfort but reduce the acuteness of the driver's vision.

If the eyes feel sore and gritty, it is better to soak clean cotton wool in a saline solution and put the wet pads on the closed lids. Eye baths are not of any great benefit, and there is a danger of transferring infection. A red or discharging eye should receive medical attention.

Middle age is a time when diseases of the eye may begin insidiously, so you should have the eyes professionally examined at regular intervals—say, every two years. Do not just wait until your vision deteriorates.

One serious disease which may occur at this time is glaucoma, a progressive increase in the tension of fluid within the eye. This affects about one person in a hundred over the age of 40. Any symptoms are noticed mostly in the evening, when dim light allows the pupils to enlarge in size. Pain may be experienced round the eye after reading and blurred vision may occur at this time, or lights are seen to have haloes round them. The eye may be very bloodshot, hard and sore to touch. The symptoms may be provoked by a heavy intake of fluid, such as drinking a few pints of beer. Coloured haloes seen round lamp posts on the way home should not be attributed to slight inebriation. Any or all of these symptoms should be reported straightaway to the doctor, so that he can arrange for specialist examination. Glaucoma is sometimes genetically determined. Anyone over 40 with a relative who is known to have glaucoma should have a screening test carried out at regular intervals so that if he has this condition it may be diagnosed at an early stage. Such a screening can be arranged by the family doctor, by referral to a hospital eye department or to an ophthalmic medical practitioner.

Some people in middle age start seeing specks that move with the movement of the eye. Normally, these are of no significance and most people who have these floaters gradually stop noticing them. They arise from a slight change in the constituents of the inner eye. However, a sudden appearance of spots before the eyes, haloes or flashes, particularly in a very short-sighted person, may be a symptom of damage to the retina and should be reported to the doctor at once, as a medical emergency.

Teeth
Eating a lot of over-refined and sugary foods is a reason why by middle age many people have lost their teeth. When the natural teeth have been replaced by dentures, the ability to chew and enjoy the taste of food is often markedly reduced, so that soft and easily managed food comes to be preferred. To have kept your own teeth in good condition to middle and late age has not only much to commend it from a cosmetic point of view, but helps to insure against many of the digestive disorders that can begin to affect us then. Good teeth working on the type of food that needs a maximum of chewing produces quantities of saliva and gets the digestive processes off to a good start.

Neglect in middle age can quite unnecessarily result in a loss of teeth. During childhood, the major disease of the teeth is decay (caries). After maturity, this becomes a less serious problem, but a more insidious condition begins to damage the teeth. The gums begin to recede and pocketing—an abnormal space developing between the tooth root and the gum—can occur. This leads both to loss of teeth and to what may be more ugly, loss of tooth-supporting bone. It is this bone loss that makes a person's face suddenly change from youthful middle age to looking old. This loss can be almost completely avoided by daily care at home and regular check-ups by your dentist.

The fundamentals of home care are to clean the teeth at least once a day, spending no less than two minutes at it. Be sure you are cleaning everywhere. Just cleaning where it is easiest can be counter-productive, since the neglected areas get decay and gum disease, while the overcleaned areas get grooves worn in them. The evidence for the efficiency of an electric toothbrush is conflicting, but if it will make you clean your teeth regularly, it is obviously useful.

As the gums slowly recede, more time should be spent cleaning the teeth. Both the decay and gum trouble appear to be caused by the dental plaque, a transparent tenacious scum of micro-organisms, enzymes, mucin from saliva and probably some food debris. The plaque gradually collects certain salts from the saliva, producing tartar. The tartar itself is relatively harmless but it produces a site for plaque which a toothbrush or toothpick cannot shift, and which only a dentist or dental hygienist can remove by regular and thorough scaling and polishing.

If the plaque is allowed to collect on any part of any tooth, it can cause decay and gingivitis (superficial inflammation of the gum margin). In older people, gingivitis may be slow and painless in onset. There is little discomfort or warning of trouble except perhaps a little bleeding when eating hard food or cleaning the teeth. This bleeding must never be ignored: go to the dentist and tell him.

Regular dental appointments every six months, even if your mouth seems healthy, but particularly if you show signs of bleeding, bad breath or loose teeth, are essential. You should go to a dentist who is prepared to take trouble with your gums and to give your teeth regular scaling.

As the February 1977 issue of *Which?* pointed out, some people wrongly assume that dental treatment comes automatically under the national health service unless they ask to be treated privately—in fact, it is the other way round. Whenever you go to a dentist, it is up to you to ask to be treated under the NHS, otherwise you may be charged as a private patient.

—cosmetic treatment

Another aspect of dental treatment that you can discuss with the dentist is what can be described as cosmetic dentistry. This is not usually available on the national health service and has to be paid for privately.

Nowadays, composite fillings made from glass or quartz in an epoxy resin are available to take the place of unsightly black or grey fillings. A great deal can be done to repair or hide ugliness caused by damage, staining or disease. Crooked teeth can be made to appear straight and, if necessary, several teeth can be crowned to give a remarkable improvement to the appearance while making no change to the character of the face, the bony structure remaining unaltered. Individual teeth that have become chipped, stained or discoloured for any reason can be crowned, though some are more difficult than others. A very loose tooth would be considered unsuitable but it may be possible for it to be crowned with an attachment to a nearby tooth which is firm, so that it will be held or splinted. This technique can save loose teeth from extraction and put off the need for dentures.

If you have lost teeth from any part of the mouth, it is wise to consider filling the gap with, for instance, a fixed bridge. Leaving a gap in the back teeth may not look ugly but can result in a loss of other teeth because you cannot chew on that side and you chew too much on the other teeth so that they get loose. Also, the teeth opposite to the gap on the same side of the mouth may over-erupt. For a bridge to be done on the national health service, approval has to be obtained by the dentist from the Dental Estimates Board.

—*dentures*

If it proves necessary for the dentist to remove all or most of the teeth and you have to have artificial dentures, it is not necessary ever to be without front teeth: modern techniques of fitting immediate dentures can avoid this. No one should wear an unaltered denture for more than about five years and a regular dental appointment should be made for a check. Bone is continually resorbed from the jaws, causing the face to fall in and the 'bite', the distance from nose to chin, to collapse. This causes problems of mastication and appearance. Building up dentures to replace lost bone can make a remarkable difference to how old a person looks. It is therefore important to have dentures built up or new ones constructed periodically.

The skin and hair

Nothing can slow down the rate of ageing, but a remarkable number of products have been designed by cosmetic firms to hide the visual effects of ageing. By the time most people reach middle age, inevitable changes in the skin and its appendages result in the formation of wrinkles, drier skin, thinning and greying of hair.

hair

Hair occurs over most of the body; the soles of the feet and palms of the hands are exceptions. There are two major types of hair: long relatively coarse terminal hair and very fine almost invisible vellus hair or fuzz. Hairs are produced in follicles (small tubules) in the skin and the thickness of the hair produced is governed by the diameter of the follicle. The hair extending above the skin surface is made up of a protein material called keratin, which is formed from cells produced at the base of the follicle. Essentially, a hair consists of an inner structure made up of keratinised cells containing a brown pigment known as melanin, overlaid by layers of thin transparent cuticle cells. The follicle has an active growing period after which the hair is shed, followed by a rest period, and then a further growing period. The growing period varies according to the type of hair; for instance, scalp, eyebrow, eyelash, beard and body hair. This accounts for the different lengths of the various types of hair of the body. Each hair follicle behaves individually and consequently hairs are not shed and replaced all at once, but a few at a time.

Attached to each hair follicle is a grease-producing gland, the sebaceous gland. The secretion (sebum) from these glands is oily and lubricates the hair shaft. There is evidence that the rate of sebum production decreases with age; this may contribute to increasing dryness of the hair and skin in middle age.

Dry hair can be caused by external abuse, such as over-bleaching, perming, colouring. Used in excess, these operations damage the structure of the hair shaft, particularly by removing the delicate cuticle cells, leaving the hair coarse and frayed. Further damage can result in splitting, not only at the end of the hair shaft but extending along the shaft. Over-enthusiastic back-combing and brushing can also cause loss of cuticle cells.

Abused hair is recognisable by its harsh strawlike texture, dryness, split ends and excessive knotting. So-called protein shampoos claim that the special materials they contain will coat and protect the hair shaft and fill in some of the indentations, in order to make the hair look more lustrous and feel thicker and smoother. A *Which?* report in February 1973 found that a laboratory test involving repeated washings of split-ended hairs from girls' heads showed no significant difference between protein and ordinary shampoos.

—colour
Hair derives its colour from the pigment melanin which forms at the base of the hair follicle. The rate of production of this pigment decreases with age, leading to at first a few hairs becoming unpigmented and later the possibility of all the hairs being unpigmented to give a head of white hair. The main factors determining the colour of hair and when it goes white are genetic.

There is no such thing as a grey hair. Human hair does not gradually fade all over from, say, black to grey but new hairs being produced unpigmented mingle with the original coloured hair to give the appearance of grey. There are some blue colour lotions on the market which can be used to neutralise the yellow tinge of 'grey' hair.

White hairs can be camouflaged by using a hair colourant. If you do this yourself, it is essential to follow the manufacturer's instructions.

Hair colourants fall basically into four categories: bleaches, rinses, semi-permanent colourant shampoos and permanent colourants. Bleaches function by penetrating the hair shaft, opening up the layers of cuticle and oxidising the natural hair pigment. The effect produced depends on the concentration of the bleaching product used, how long it stays in contact and at what temperature. Bleaching is normally carried out immediately after the hair has been shampooed and dried. The bleach is added on strands gradually covering the whole head. The process can be stopped when the hair looks the desired colour, by copious rinsing with water and the rinsing agent supplied by the manufacturer.

Colour rinses are temporary colours which are poured over the head. They simply coat the outer hair shaft without actually penetrating and are washed out by shampooing. A rinse can effectively cover up small amounts of white hairs particularly if they are well distributed; the drawback is that by coating the hair some of the natural sheen of the hair is lost.

Colourant shampoos are generally semi-permanent dyes which remain on the hair through several shampooings. They are useful for covering up white hairs and are also often used for highlighting the hair. Colourant shampoos are normally applied by washing the hair with shampoo in the normal way, and then leaving the second lather to remain on the hair until the desired tint has been achieved. The colouring in the shampoo is not just one dye, but a number. If one of the dyes in the tint is preferentially absorbed by the hair shaft, a predominance of this colour will occur which could produce quite unexpected results. This is why it is important to carry out a trial on some hairs first; also to determine the length of time necessary to produce the desired depth of shade. Over-bleaching or perming greatly increases the porosity of the hair and hair that has been so treated will require less time to take up the shade than normal untreated hair.

Permanent hair colourants (sometimes called oxidation colourants) when applied properly can yield natural-looking shades. As the name implies, they cannot be washed out by shampooing. If dissatisfied with the shade, you have to wait for it to grow out, or bleach and retint until the desired shade is achieved.

Permanent dyeing of the hair should never be undertaken before a skin test with the product is made. This can be done by putting a small dab of the solution to be used either behind the ear or on the forearm not less than twenty-four hours before it is intended to colour the hair. If this produces any redness or irritation, it means that the skin is sensitive to one of the materials in the colourant and this type of colourant should not be used. Permanent dyeing of the hair is best left to an expert hairdresser.

In September 1975 *Which?* said in reply to people who had written concerning newspaper reports about cancer risks with permanent and semi-permanent hair colourants, and wanted to know whether they should stop using these dyes: 'The position is that some studies with bacteria in the USA and the UK have shown that common ingredients of these preparations can affect bacterial cells in a way that known carcinogenic substances do. However, work on animals, to detect carcinogenic effects, has not yet found much. Until this work is completed, we cannot say whether there actually is a risk. Meanwhile all you can do if you are really worried about it, is stop using hair dyes altogether. There is not a complete list of the brands containing the chemical under suspicion, and, anyway, other chemicals used in dyes might also be suspect. A situation like this underlines the need for regulations about the contents of cosmetics.' Results of more recent tests, with human beings, have not disproved the potential risk.

—loss

Some thinning of the hair and partial loss of hair is normal with increasing age. Excessive thinning of the hair, however, may be a result of ill health or scalp disorder, and you should consult your doctor.

Baldness (alopecia) or thinning of the hair associated with ageing can be due to permanent loss of functioning hair follicles, or to new hairs being thinner than those which have been shed.

Permanent loss of hair from the top, front and back of the head is called male pattern baldness. Genetic factors and the activity of male hormones affect the degee and onset of loss of hair. It can occur at any age, from twenty onwards. Some older women, too, get some degree of male pattern baldness due to changes in their hormonal balance after the menopause.

Male baldness, to a certain extent, is hereditary. Many treatments have been suggested for the prevention of baldness and many so-called cures are on sale, but short of grafting skin which contains active follicles on to the scalp, no method is reliable or has any scientific basis.

Although baldness in women is rare, the hair may get generally thinner. A temporary bulking-out of thinning hair can be achieved by the use of conditioners, setting lotions or sprays. These products contain various additives such as resins and proteins to build up the hair shaft, giving an illusion of thicker hair.

—unwanted

Superfluous hair has plagued women throughout the ages. When it becomes troublesome after the menopause, it is thought that it may be due to a change in the balance of sex hormones in the bloodstream. Fine hair starts to become obvious on areas such as the chin and upper lip and the cheek; frequently the hair on the legs becomes thicker. Shaving does not change fine hair into coarse terminal hair or affect the rate of growth, toughness or colour, as is often thought. But because it has been cut only at the skin surface leaving the growing area in the follicle untouched, hair soon reappears as short stubble which, because of its length, appears tougher and thicker than the original hair.

Unwanted hair can be removed by depilatories which act by chemical degradation of the protein of the hair shaft. Depilatories generally give a longer lasting effect than shaving because they destroy the hair farther down the follicle. They come as creams, liquids and pastes, in different forms and strengths, and it is important to use them correctly and only on the part of the body recommended by the manufacturer. Some people are sensitive to the materials used in these products. Before using a chemical depilatory, apply it to a small area of skin, leaving it on for ten minutes; only if no signs of redness or irritation appear can you consider the product safe for your skin.

Wax depilatories remove hairs by pulling the hardened wax off against the direction of hair growth. They should not be used in the armpit region or over warts, moles or abraded skin.

Hair can also be removed by a process known as electrolysis. A needle is introduced into the hair follicle, and a high-frequency alternating current put through it to destroy the growing area of follicle. Each hair to be removed has to be treated individually and the process is consequently time-consuming and costly. Success depends on regular treatment, the use of modern equipment and skilled operating technique. The number of times regrowth has to be treated depends on the extent of growth, strength of hair, type of skin and previous treatments. Regrowth after electrolysis becomes progressively weaker. No matter how much treatment a person undergoes, it will be to no avail unless the operator works carefully and accurately. Cleanliness, the sterility of the equipment and accuracy are essential to avoid infection and possible scarring.

skin

The skin provides a protective barrier and conserves the body's moisture. It houses numerous nerve endings and contains sweat glands and various other structures such as fat cells, blood vessels, sebaceous glands, hair follicles.

The skin basically consists of a lower layer known as the dermis, with a thinner and tougher outer layer, the epidermis. The dermis makes up the bulk of skin and essentially comprises collagen (a relatively inert fibrous protein) and elastic fibres in a complex gel-like substance. This arrangement allows the skin to be strong yet non-rigid and to adjust accurately to the shape of objects closely in contact with it.

The amount of dermis decreases with age and the subcutaneous tissue (a layer of fat underlying the dermis) becomes thinner. The collagen itself alters on ageing becoming more cross-linked and therefore more rigid and less elastic. Also, collagen changes on exposure to ultraviolet rays from the sun: the greater the exposure, the greater the degeneration of the collagen fibres.

The cumulative effect is a slow but definite loss in the elasticity of the dermis and, more important, a lessening of the ability of the skin to adjust to long-term changes in the underlying tissue. Wrinkles therefore appear. In sunny climates and outdoor workers, skin wrinkling occurs up to ten years sooner than in duller climates. Most nuns, for example, have few wrinkles even when quite old. So if you want to keep a good skin—stay out of the sun.

The outstanding characteristic of ageing skin is its loss of elasticity; cosmetics can have only a relatively small effect in counteracting the process.

Face masks or mud packs can reduce wrinkles temporarily. The old-fashioned mud pack was mixed with water, applied to the face and allowed to dry. As the clay dried, it contracted, producing a noticeable tightening effect on the skin for a while. Modern face packs are clear liquids which form a thin film over the surface of the skin and when completely dry can be peeled off. The idea is that the film acts as a barrier to prevent moisture in the epidermis escaping to the atmosphere, so as to give a temporary rosy plumpness to the skin.

There are data to suggest that local application of oestrogen in sufficient concentration affects the water-holding capacity of the skin, and medical treatment with oestrogen tablets for menopausal symptoms may have an associated effect on the skin.

—dry skin
Dry skin, which becomes increasingly common as people grow older, is basically associated with the epidermis, the outer layer of the skin.

The flexibility of the skin is dependent on the water content of the epidermis, particularly the outermost horny layer which must contain at least ten per cent by weight to remain soft. Water migrates upwards from the deeper dermal tissues or comes from sweat, or is taken from the atmosphere and from water or aqueous preparations applied to the skin.

The skin of an older person has a greatly decreased capacity for taking up and holding water. This is believed by some to be due to a deficiency in certain hygroscopic (water-absorbing) substances in the skin. Normally, oily secretions prevent these from escaping when the skin is washed. This oiliness is lost by excessive immersion of the skin in water and detergents. As the activity of the sebaceous glands and sweat glands alters during the ageing process, the rate of sebum production diminishes so that the skin's capacity to hold moisture is reduced, resulting in drier skin in middle and old age.

The superficial roughness and scaling of dry skin may result in a tightening or cracking of the skin, and itching. If nothing is done about it, severe dryness can lead to fissuring and painful inflammation.

To prevent dry skin getting worse, take normal precautions such as using gloves for household chores and drying the skin thoroughly after washing.

Protect the skin, where possible, from excessive exposure to wind or cold, and try to avoid a very dry atmosphere such as occurs in some centrally heated offices. These factors cause moisture to be lost from the skin by evaporation, leading to drying out of the skin surface, hardening and roughening. If you have a tendency to dry skin, use of a good skin cream or hand lotion should become a habit.

In a report on moisturisers in January 1976 *Which?* said 'Putting fatty, oily or waxy stuff on the skin smooths and cements down any flakes, making the surface feel soft, and helping to delay the evaporation of moisture. So mixtures of oils and water (emulsions) should soften and smooth the skin and prevent rapid moisture loss. And that is basically all that moisturisers, cold creams and many other skin creams are.'

—face lift
The effect of cosmetics on wrinkles or sagging skin is only transitory. This is accepted by the majority of women but some are so concerned about the appearance of their ageing skin that they want to resort to plastic surgery.

Most of the operations carried out by plastic surgeons in hospitals are for people suffering from burns, road accidents, skin diseases and abnormalities of the features. People requesting cosmetic surgery purely for aesthetic reasons and renewal of youth are not usually eligible for treatment under the national health service unless the change in appearance has caused emotional disturbance which places the general health of the person in jeopardy. Otherwise, one has to go as a fee-paying patient to a hospital or nursing home. The cost of cosmetic surgery is high, and varies according to circumstances.

A face lift generally requires a stay in hospital of about one week. In the usual operation, incisions are made inside the hairline, the skin is then stretched upward and outward, thereby removing wrinkles, lines and any sagginess of the skin. The incision heals rapidly and within four weeks is hardly noticeable—a suitable hairstyle would cover any fine scars remaining. Techniques in cosmetic surgery have improved over the years and the after-look of a face lift no longer has a taut unnatural mask-like appearance.

The skin gradually becomes slack again and the rejuvenating effect may last for only five or six years, depending on the individual, the natural elasticity of the skin, the manner in which the skin is treated and the environment. It is possible to have a second face-lifting operation later, but the same incision lines have to be used; a third face lift would be difficult.

A face lift will not remove deep forehead frown lines or bags under the eyes. These have to be treated as a separate operation (which may be carried out at the same time). Bags under the eyes caused by excess subcutaneous tissue can be removed without scarring and the effect is permanent.

Many small blemishes and lumps appear in ageing skin and may cause cosmetic embarrassment. Most of these are harmless, but any spot which bleeds or increases in size or gets sore, should be examined by a doctor in case it needs removing.

nails

A healthy finger nail normally grows at the rate of a fraction of a millimetre a day, taking five to six months to grow from the matrix to the nail tip; a toe nail takes about 18 months. (Often, splitting or flaking of the free edge of the nail is attributed to, say, a coincidental change in nail varnish remover, whereas it is more likely caused by factors which affected the matrix some months previously.) The rate of nail growth slows with age and there may be associated thickening and opacities.

White spots appearing on the nail (leukonychia) are not due to lack of calcium in the diet. The nail plate is translucent and only appears pink due to the underlying blood vessels in the nail bed. If the nail suffers some form of trauma, such as knocking, squeezing, nail-biting or over-enthusiastic use of a nail file in pushing back the cuticle, the nail plate lifts from the nail bed in the area of the injury, forming pockets of air. The whiteness is due to refraction of light through the air pockets in the nail and they grow out with the nail.

Some diseases lead to changes in the nails: for instance, anaemia can lead to thinning and softening of the nail plate, which may become concave. The cause of brittle nails is not understood; sometimes it is due to disease but it may be caused by nail varnish.

When the fingers or toes feel cold and go numb, this is an indication of a temporary restriction of the blood flow. The nail matrix and nail bed are well supplied with blood vessels, but situated as they are at the end of the digits, they are vulnerable to vascular spasm. More permanent restriction interferes with the formation of the nail plate and can lead to thinning, splitting, and longitudinal ridging of the nail.

Feet

In middle age, the feet often begin to show the effects of the indignities they suffered during earlier years by being crammed into unsuitable shoes. Being overweight causes additional load to be placed on the feet, and some local aches and pains may be due to this.

By middle age, there is bound to be some degree of osteoarthrosis, a degenerative disorder of joints, which may gradually reduce the former mobility of the feet. Footwear should be chosen to allow for the changes that are taking place: for example, a wider fitting shoe may now be needed for comfort and to relieve pressure.

Toes may show the effects of pressure from footwear and may even have become hammer toes due to being held bunched together, and be unable to work properly. The little toe may have burrowed under the fourth toe, making the joint at the base of the little toe more pronounced and subject to pressure. Limitation of movement in the toes leads to the formation of corns or callosities, not only on the toes but also on the ball of the foot. Painful corns and callosities should be treated by a qualified chiropodist (state registered chiropodists have the letters SRCh after their name). The chiropodist can also advise on adapting footwear to allow for deformed toes and joints.

Many middle-aged women have pronounced hallux valgus or a bunion joint, a condition where the big toe has deviated towards the other toes, making the joint at the base of the big toe much more prominent. This condition, which may well have started in earlier years, insidiously gets worse. There may by now be some limitation of movement of the joint. Some people develop a true bunion—this is inflammation of the protective sac of fluid which forms over the joint as a reaction to pressure from the shoe. In most cases of hallux valgus, all that can be done is to make the foot more comfortable by wearing shoes that protect it from pressure. Hallux valgus can be operated on but the results are often not completely satisfactory.

Some obese women develop intractable hyperkeratosis (masses of thick skin) on the soles and around the heels of the feet, often with painful cracks and fissures. The bulk of the thick skin can be reduced by a chiropodist. Putting on an emollient such as hand cream, after washing the feet, makes the skin more pliable and helps to alleviate some of the discomfort. If the fissures have opened, the cream used should be antiseptic. Hyperkeratosis, which may be associated with the menopause, can occur also on other parts of the body, such as the palms of the hands or the knees, and may respond to hormone treatment.

Prominent veins sometimes occur on the feet, but alone are not of great significance. Varicose veins in the legs can be a cause of oedema (swelling) due to fluid accumulating in the feet. There are many other causes of oedema—for example, heart or kidney disease—and the swelling of the feet is a manifestation of the underlying condition, for which medical advice should be sought.

Sometimes a painful sensation is experienced in and around the fourth toe when walking. It varies from a tingling burning sensation to sudden pain shooting from the foot into the toes. When the pain comes on, the sufferer, usually a woman, has to stop walking, remove her shoe and massage the foot. Sometimes the area aches for a long time after the attack of sharp pain has subsided. This condition, called plantar digital neuritis, stems from the nerves that pass to the toes becoming compressed by the adjacent bones, or the blood supply to the nerve being inter-rupted. In many cases, the pain is triggered off by a particular pair of shoes and does not occur with a different type of shoe—for example, a lace-up one in place of a slip-on casual. If the condition persists, however, ask the doctor or chiropodist about it.

Middle-aged men, especially if of ample proportions, sometimes develop a painful area beneath the heel. There is often difficulty in making an accurate diagnosis of this tiresome condition. It may be due to repeated minor damage to the fibrous structure attached to the heel bone—a condition called plantar fasciitis. Damage to this area may result in a bony projection forming on the heel bone; however, these can occur on heels without pain. A sponge pad placed in the heel of the shoe to act as a shock absorber in walking often gives some relief to painful heel conditions. Persistent pain in the heel should be reported to your doctor.

B

Aspects of health

Middle age represents just one phase in the continuous process of maturing and growing older. It is a time of challenge to maintain former fitness and drive. The years do not of themselves imply a lower standard of health.

A person's physical status in middle life is affected by his earlier life and upbringing; how much consideration he gives to his health; what kind of work he does; how well he has adapted to other people; whether he smokes or drinks or takes drugs such as sedatives. The middle-aged man who wants to improve his health prospects must look to see where there is room for manoeuvre in his life-style. Influences, attitudes and habits are capable of being changed, or at least modified. Many troubles are due to imposing on the body the problems of dealing with stress, lack of exercise, cigarette smoking, the wrong foods or too much food.

weight
The data collected by life insurance companies show that life expectancy decreases with fatness. If you are overweight, you run a greater risk of developing certain diseases, such as diabetes, gallstones, heart attacks, high blood pressure, and some forms of arthritis. Being overweight means more wear and tear on your joints and ligaments and this can result in more aches and pains. If you need an operation (for example, a hip replacement later), the risk of possible complications will be greater and the surgeon may well ask you to lose weight before he attempts surgery.

Both men and women tend to increase in weight in their forties and fifties. However, middle-aged spread cannot be excused on the grounds that it is something that is bound to happen as one gets older. It is a reflection of the extra fat that the body has been allowed to lay down over the years. The fat deposits which are the largest when young seem to be the ones to gain most fat during ageing; the smallest deposits gain least.

There is an adage that 'men run to tum and women to bum' and this has been scientifically confirmed by measuring the thickness of fat at different sites in men and women of different ages. Since young men of normal height and weight usually have a greater proportion of fat around their middle, this is where the new fat will be deposited. Women, who usually have more of their fat around their buttocks and upper thighs, find that these are usually the areas affected by the spread. Around the time of the menopause, there seems to be a slight change in the pattern and the spread moves towards the trunk and away from the upper thighs.

It seems, therefore, that you do not have much control over where your fat is deposited. However, whether fat is deposited at all is under your control.

The reasons for a tendency to deposit fat with age are mainly a decline in energy expenditure and/or an increase in the intake of food and drink, resulting in an energy intake which is larger than the energy output. The body will store any surplus as fat.

A person's total energy expenditure is made up of a voluntary and an involuntary component. The involuntary component is the energy needed to keep the body functioning correctly—for blood circulation, respiration, digestion, and so on. This component varies from one person to another but remains reasonably constant throughout life. It may go down very slightly because there tends to be a small decrease in the amount of muscle in most people after the age of about 30.

A GUIDE TO YOUR WEIGHT
(all weights without clothes; heights without shoes)

	height		weight range				
	ft	*in*	*st*	*lb*		*st*	*lb*
MEN	5	1	7	7	*to*	9	2
	5	2	7	10		9	6
	5	3	7	13		9	9
	5	4	8	1		9	13
	5	5	8	5		10	2
	5	6	8	8		10	7
	5	7	8	12		10	12
	5	8	9	2		11	2
	5	9	9	5		11	7
	5	10	9	9		11	12
	5	11	10	0		12	3
	6	0	10	4		12	7
	6	1	10	8		12	12
	6	2	10	12		13	4
	6	3	11	3		13	9
WOMEN	4	8	6	3	*to*	7	8
	4	9	6	5		7	11
	4	10	6	8		8	0
	4	11	6	11		8	4
	5	0	6	13		8	7
	5	1	7	2		8	10
	5	2	7	5		9	0
	5	3	7	8		9	4
	5	4	7	12		9	9
	5	5	8	2		9	13
	5	6	8	5		10	4
	5	7	8	9		10	8
	5	8	8	13		10	12
	5	9	9	2		11	3
	5	10	9	6		11	7

1 ft = 30·5 cm	1 st = 6·35 kg
1 in = 2·5 cm	1 lb = 0·45 kg

The voluntary component, however, is likely to show great variation throughout life. It is determined by the amount of exercise taken—for example, standing needs more energy than sitting, walking more than standing, running more than walking. If when you were younger you were much more active, walking to and from work rather than sitting in your car or on a train, you would then have used more energy than you do now. However, this does not mean that middle age is the time of life to take up weightlifting. But when one's occupation and activities use brains more than muscles, food requirements must be reassessed downwards because the energy requirements are considerably less. So the man who drives a car, sits in the office all day, and remains chairbound in the evening watching television, needs to be careful about how much and what he eats.

The change in a person's pattern of life need not be dramatic to cause a swing towards a greater intake of energy through food than output through taking exercise. A man can gradually put on about 20 lb in the course of ten years if his energy intake exceeds output by only a small plain biscuit a day. If you no longer take a regular 20-minute walk to the station, say, you should replace it with some other energy-using activity, or at least do not use the extra 20 minutes for eating another piece of toast and marmalade—or even that small plain biscuit.

The table (taken from the book *Which? way to slim*) gives an indication of weights for different heights. For each height, there is an appropriate range based on average desirable weights for different body frame sizes. If your weight falls well within this range, you need not worry about it. If it is at the top of the range or above it, you should watch your weight carefully and try to reduce it before it creeps higher, because you would be medically at risk.

Keep a careful eye on your weight at all times. Mirrors, clothes and scales are your best checks. Do not just accept that you need a larger dress or trouser size every time you buy new ones. Use this as a warning signal and try to be able to return to your original size. If possible, weigh yourself without clothing regularly on the same scales. Write down your weight somewhere so that you cannot conveniently forget it—a diary is a good place. When your weight goes up, it is because you have been eating and drinking too much or taking too little exercise. People who expect to lose weight by doing exercises alone are rarely successful. It is more effective and probably safer for a middle-aged person to cut the intake of food and drink. Reduce your intake until your weight returns to normal and then make sure that you keep it there either by taking more exercise and increasing your energy output, or by keeping a careful watch on what you eat, particularly those second helpings. You will find it much easier to take off a couple of pounds of fat which has only just been formed than a stone of fat that has taken up permanent residence.

losing weight
The best way of ridding yourself of surplus fat is to control eating and drinking in such a way that your body has to call on its fat stores to supply you with energy. Energy is measured in calories; the calorific value of foods is expressed in kilocalories (abbreviated to kcal or Calorie). With the international system of units being introduced, energy is measured in joules: 4·2 kilojoules = 1 Calorie. Every surplus pound of fat represents an energy store of about 3500 Calories. So, to get rid of a pound of fat, you must use up 3500 Calories more than you take in.

To do this, you must have a rough idea of the amount of energy you use up during a normal day. A middle-aged man who is moderately active expends between 2600 Calories and 3600 Calories, approximately, a day; a woman, between 2200 and 2500. Running or playing squash takes about twice as many calories as walking quite fast, ballroom dancing twice as many as cricket. In order to lose weight at a reasonable rate, you should aim at a daily deficit of about 1000 Calories. So, a typist should aim at an intake of only about 1200 Calories and a man who does heavy manual work should aim at an intake of no more than 2600 Calories.

In order to know enough about the food you eat to be able to stick to the number of calories that you have allowed yourself, you will need a table of calorie values showing the number of calories in most of the common foods and drinks. The number of calories in a particular food depends on the amount of fat, carbohydrate, protein and water that it contains. Fat contains about twice as many calories per ounce as protein or carbohydrate; water is calorie-free. Therefore, foods which contain a lot of water (such as cucumber) have relatively low calorie values compared with foods which contain a lot of fat.

To get used to being aware of calorie values, write down what you have eaten and drunk and at the end of the day, work out the total number of calories consumed. This total will probably be above the number of calories that you have decided to allow yourself in order to lose weight. So you must examine the list carefully and then decide where you can make the best calorie savings, by cutting out certain foods or by substituting low-calorie foods for high-calorie ones. If, for example, you eat a lot of cheddar cheese, either you can cut down the amount you eat or you can try eating curd cheese or cottage cheese instead—weight for weight these contain only about a third of the calories in cheddar cheese because of their lower fat content.

The normal diet in this country contains carbohydrate, fat, protein, minerals and vitamins.

Carbohydrates—sugar and starchy foods such as bread, potatoes, rice—are not strictly essential; their use is mainly to provide energy. Sugar is the slimmer's worst enemy because it is virtually 100 per cent carbohydrate.

Fats have an important dietary role as well as providing a concentrated energy store. Sources of fat are butter, margarine, milk, oils, cheese.

Protein is an essential part of the diet because it is from protein that worn tissues in the body are replaced. Sources of protein are meat, eggs, fish, cheese, milk, some cereals and pulses.

When deciding what to cut out or cut down on, you should bear in mind that your final diet should not lack any important vitamins and minerals. If at least a third of your calories comes from foods such as meat, fish, eggs or cheese, which are high in vitamins and minerals as well as in protein, this should ensure that you will not have any deficiencies in your diet.

Calories and food

note stewed fruit is without sugar
   fish includes skin and bones; cooked without fat
alcoholic drinks: spirits, liqueurs = standard pub measure ($\frac{1}{6}$ gill; 0·83 fl oz)
         port, sherry = standard pub measure ($\frac{1}{3}$ gill, 1·66 fl oz)
         wine = medium glass ($\frac{1}{6}$ bottle; 4·4 fl oz)

Calorie ranges
under 10
1 oz cabbage, raw
8 oz celery, boiled
3 oz chicory, raw
3 oz cucumber, raw
3 oz lettuce
4 oz mushrooms, raw or grilled
   without fat
3 oz mustard and cress
8 oz rhubarb, stewed

1 cup bovril (1 tsp)
negligible:
low-calorie drinks
1 cup coffee (no milk or sugar)
1 cup tea (no milk or sugar)
none:
water

10–20
8 oz runner beans, boiled
4 oz broccoli tops, boiled
6 oz cabbage, boiled
6 oz cauliflower, boiled
6 oz (3 sticks) celery, raw
4 oz gooseberries, stewed
5 oz ($\frac{1}{2}$ medium) grapefruit
6 oz spring greens, boiled
8 oz marrow, boiled
4 oz (1 medium slice) melon
4 oz onion, boiled
4 oz radishes
4 oz tomatoes, raw or grilled
6 oz turnips, boiled
4 oz watercress

1 glass (5 fl oz) lemon juice,
   unsweetened
1 cup marmite (1 tsp)
1 cup oxo (1 cube)

20–30
4 oz fresh apricots, raw or
   stewed
2 oz (1 medium) beetroot,
   boiled
4 oz blackberries, stewed
4 oz blackcurrants, stewed
4 oz carrots
$\frac{1}{2}$ oz fish paste
4 oz leeks, boiled
1 oz olives
2 oz spring onion, raw
2 oz (1 medium slice) fresh
   pineapple
4 oz plums, stewed
4 oz raspberries, raw or stewed
4 oz spinach, boiled
5 oz sprouts, boiled
4 oz strawberries
5 oz swedes, boiled
2 tangerines (4 oz)

1 cup coffee (+ milk)
1 cup tea (+ milk)
1 glass (5 fl oz) tomato juice

Calorie ranges

30–40
4 oz blackberries, raw
4 oz damsons, raw or stewed
½ oz jam
½ oz marmalade
½ oz mincemeat
1 medium peach (4 oz)
1 medium pear (4 oz), raw or
   stewed

2 tbs squash: lemon, lime

40–50
1 eating apple (4 oz)
4 oz broad beans, boiled
¼ oz cheese spread
4 oz cherries, raw or stewed
½ oz golden syrup
4 oz greengages, stewed
½ oz honey
½ oz lemon curd
1 medium orange (5 oz)
2 oz pineapple, tinned
4 oz plums, raw
2 oz tomatoes, fried
½ pt clear soup (up to 65
   Calories)

2 tbs squash: grapefruit, orange

50–60
6 oz apple, stewed
1 small slice bread
4 oz greengages, raw
½ oz parmesan cheese

4 oz peas, fresh or frozen,
   cooked
4 oz plaice
4 oz sole
2 oz sweetcorn, boiled

1 glass (5 fl oz) apple juice
1 glass (5 fl oz) grapefruit juice,
   unsweetened
1 glass dry sherry
1 glass spirits (gin, rum, vodka,
   whisky)
1 glass dry vermouth

60–70
1 baked apple (6 oz)
4 oz dried apricots, stewed
1 banana, medium (5 oz)
2 tbs single cream (1 fl oz)
2 oz cottage cheese
4 oz grapes
2 oz ham
4 oz parsnips, boiled
¼ pt porridge (made with water)
2 oz prawns
2 oz shrimps
½ pt thin soup (up to 100
   Calories)

1 glass brandy
½ pt fizzy lemonade
1 liqueur (up to 90 Calories)
1 cup (6 fl oz) milk from low-fat
   skimmed powder
1 glass (5 fl oz) orange juice,
   unsweetened
1 glass sweet sherry

Calorie ranges

70–80
2 oz crab
4 oz fish: cod, haddock, lemon sole, turbot, whiting
4 oz mandarin oranges, tinned
4 oz dried prunes, stewed
4 oz spaghetti, tinned (in tomato sauce)
5 oz (1 carton) plain low-fat yogurt

1 glass (5 fl oz) pineapple juice, unsweetened
1 glass port
1 glass sweet vermouth

80–90
2 oz curd cheese
4 oz pears, tinned

90–100
1 egg, boiled or poached
4 oz fish: hake, trout
4 oz jelly
1 baked potato (4 oz)
2 medium potatoes, boiled (4 oz)
$\frac{1}{2}$ pt thick soup (up to 200 Calories)
4 oz strawberries, tinned

1 can (11$\frac{1}{2}$ fl oz) tonic water
1 glass dry wine

100–110
4 oz baked beans, or haricot or butter beans (boiled)
1 slice bread from large loaf (1$\frac{1}{2}$ oz)
2 fish fingers (2 oz)
4 oz fruit salad, tinned
4 oz lentils, boiled
4 oz peaches, tinned
2 oz salmon, smoked

$\frac{1}{2}$ pt dry cider
1 fl oz condensed milk

110–120
4 oz halibut
2 oz (small block) ice cream
1 fl oz salad cream
3 oz salmon, tinned
1 level tbs sugar (1 oz)
4 oz tripe, stewed

1 cup coffee, all milk
1 can (11$\frac{1}{2}$ fl oz) bitter lemon
1 can (11$\frac{1}{2}$ fl oz) shandy
1 glass sweet wine

Calorie ranges

120–130
4 oz apricots, tinned
$\frac{1}{2}$ avocado pear (5 oz)
2 biscuits, plain (1 oz)
3 slices corned beef (2 oz)
4 oz dried figs, stewed
4 oz macaroni, boiled
2 oz mushrooms, fried
4 oz spaghetti, boiled
2 rashers streaky bacon, grilled
  (1 oz)

$\frac{1}{2}$ pt sweet cider
1 can (11$\frac{1}{2}$ fl oz) cola

130–140
2 tbs double cream (1 fl oz)
2 oz currants
4 fl oz custard (+ milk and
  sugar)
1 egg, fried
4 oz boiled ham, lean

1 cup cocoa (+ milk)

140–150
2 rashers streaky bacon, fried
  (1 oz)
3 fish fingers (3 oz)
1 egg omelette
2 oz raisins
1 cupful rice, boiled (4 oz)
4 oz semolina or sago pudding
2 oz sultanas
5 oz (1 carton) fruit yogurt

1 pt draught mild

150–160
1 oz short crust pastry
1 oz potato crisps

1 pt lager

160–170
2 sweet biscuits (1 oz)
1 oz cereal (+ milk)
4 oz roast chicken
1 oz muesli (+ milk)
1 oz flaky pastry
4 oz rice pudding
4 oz roast turkey

1 pt brown ale
1 cup malted drink (+ milk)

170–180
2 rashers back bacon, grilled
  (1$\frac{1}{2}$ oz)
2 oz brie cheese
2 oz camembert cheese
2 oz edam cheese
4 oz lamb's kidney, fried
2 slices lean roast beef (4 oz)
2 oz liver sausage
1 oz peanut butter

180–190
6 oz baked kipper
3 oz grilled steak
3 oz pilchards, tinned, in sauce
4 oz salmon, fresh

1 pt pale ale
1 pt draught bitter
1 cup chocolate (+ milk)
$\frac{1}{2}$ pint fresh milk

Calorie ranges

190–200
2 slices gammon, grilled (3 oz)
2 oz gouda cheese
3 oz sweetbreads, fried

200–210
1 medium slice cake (up to 300 Calories)
1 oz cereal (+ milk and sugar)
2 oz danish blue cheese
1 egg scrambled (+ milk and fat)
3 oz roast lamb's heart
2 oz onion, fried
4 oz rabbit, stewed
3 slices roast leg of pork, lean (4 oz)

1 pt bottled stout

210–220
2 oz cheese, processed
2 slices lean roast beef (sirloin) (4 oz)
3 slices roast leg of lamb, lean (4 oz)
2 medium roast potatoes (4 oz)

220–230
1 oz butter
2 oz cheshire cheese
3 oz chipped potatoes
2 oz cob nuts
2 oz gorgonzola cheese
1 oz margarine

230–240
2 rashers back bacon, grilled (2 oz)
6 oz mackerel, fried
2 oz stilton cheese
2 oz wensleydale cheese

1 cup cocoa (+ milk and sugar)

240–250
2 oz cheddar cheese
4 oz dates
4 oz figs
4 oz grilled steak
2 rashers streaky bacon, grilled (2 oz)
2 oz toffees
4 oz veal cutlet, fried (egg and breadcrumbed)

250–260
6 oz roast chicken
3 oz sardines, tinned
3 oz tuna, tinned

260–270
2 rashers back bacon, fried (2 oz)
2 oz chocolates
1 oz cooking fat
1 oz cooking oil
2 oz cream cheese
2 oz gruyère cheese
3 oz luncheon meat

Calorie ranges

270–280
4 oz boiled salt beef
1 croissant

280–300
4 oz calf liver, fried
4 oz stewed lamb

300–320
6 oz boiled chicken
2 oz bar plain chocolate
4 oz tinned chopped ham
3 slices roast leg of lamb (4 oz)
2 large beef sausages (4 oz)
2 oz walnuts

320–340
2 oz bar milk chocolate
3 slices roast leg of pork (4 oz)
4 oz grilled sprats
4 oz tongue

340–360
2 oz almonds
2 oz desiccated coconut
2 slices roast duck (4 oz)
6 oz herring, fried in oatmeal
2 oz peanuts

360–380
2 oz brazil nuts
6 oz grilled steak
2 large pork sausages (4 oz)
3 slices roast shoulder of lamb
(4 oz)

380–400
6 oz grilled gammon
6 oz minced beef
6 oz stewed steak

400++
6 oz fish fried in breadcrumbs
1 large lamb chop (6 oz)
8 oz grilled steak
1 pizza

> *ounces: grammes*
> $1\ oz = 28 \cdot 4\ g$
> $100\ g = 3\frac{1}{2}\ oz$

The figures on pages 35 to 40 are based on those in *Which? way to slim*

Once you have started to limit your calorie intake, you should begin to see your weight dropping. You will probably lose more weight during the first week than during subsequent weeks. Before your body starts breaking down its main energy reserves of fat, it has another minor source of energy to call on: glycogen which is stored in the liver and muscles. More water is released from the breaking down of glycogen than of fat. So your initial loss of weight during, say, the first week on a diet, is likely to be greater than the weight you lose after that.

The human body is made up of over 60 per cent water. (Six stone of a 10-stone person is therefore accounted for by water.) This water is essential: no one can survive for more than a few days without fluid whereas most people could live for several weeks without food. Fluid retention cannot be made the scapegoat for being overweight, but does play a part in the normal fluctuation of weight in a woman. During her monthly cycle, the levels of oestrogen and progesterone in the blood can influence the amount of water that is retained. On average, women weigh two or three pounds more in the few days before menstruation, due to extra water. However, this can vary; some women do not gain any weight, some gain as much as four pounds.

The amount of fluid that the body retains depends much more on hormonal balance than on the amount of fluid that is drunk. Some slimming diets restrict the amount of water to be drunk during the day. There is no need for this; provided your kidneys are functioning adequately, your body will retain the amount of fluid that is essential and get rid of the excess through its normal channels.

Fluid retention can explain the seemingly massive increase in weight that slimmers often experience if they suddenly have an eating binge after several days of deprivation, especially if the binge includes lots of sugar and starches (high in carbohydrate). This will immediately fill up your glycogen stores which you had previously depleted, and the pointer on your bathroom scales may shoot up several pounds due to the extra water you store with the glycogen. Eating carefully for a couple of days, especially avoiding sugar and starches, will soon deplete these stores again and you will be back on your downward trend.

Many of the commercial low-calorie preparations, such as sugar substitutes and low-fat spreads, can help, provided you count their calories. There are also a number of substitute meals which specify the number of Calories per biscuit or serving.

The correct way to slim is not by losing a large amount in a short time but by reforming your eating habits on a long-term basis.

Very severe dieting should only be carried out under medical supervision so that a check can be kept to see that no deficiency arises and that essential proteins, minerals and vitamins are included.

There are drugs, obtainable on prescription, for suppressing the appetite. However, they have side effects which include nervousness, excitability, difficulty in sleeping or difficulty in staying awake, depression. The appetite-suppressant effect begins to wear off after a time and some such drugs are habit-forming and can lead to dependence. There is increasing reluctance on the part of doctors to prescribe appetite-suppressing drugs.

Control of weight is a question of balancing intake of food and output of energy, and requires a degree of personal insight and a good deal of resolution to succeed. If the motivation is strong enough to succeed, reducing weight can be an exhilarating experience as one begins to feel more energetic and more youthful.

Diet and diseases

Not only excessive eating has its dangers; deficiencies in our modern diet also can lead to disease. It is only recently that our changing dietary habits have been linked with the increase in certain diseases which were formerly rare, and which scarcely occur in other parts of the world with a different diet where the pattern of eating has not changed. There is much evidence to show that diseases such as diabetes, peptic ulcer, hiatus hernia, obesity, appendicitis, gall bladder disease, diverticulitis, coronary disease, have increased significantly in western countries but are almost unknown in underdeveloped countries.

Apart from the enormous increase in the consumption of sugar and fats in our diet, the greatest change that has occurred in the nature of our food is the reduction of its vegetable fibre content. This coincided with the introduction of refined (low extraction) flour in the 1880s, and consequent loss of fibre in bread. The bowels behave differently with an over-refined diet than a diet in which the fibre content is high. Adequate fibre in the diet produces a bulkier and better formed stool and shortens the transit time through the intestine. The pressure that builds up against the wall of the intestinal canal is therefore reduced, as is the activity of the bacteria growing within the gut. Natural fibres are thought by some experts to prevent the production of harmful degradation products and to prevent these from concentrating for long periods in contact with the lining membrane of the bowel (a possible factor in producing bowel diseases such as diverticulitis or even cancer). Adding bran to the diet, eating wholemeal bread, coarse green vegetables, salads and unpeeled fruit, all help to provide fibre in the diet.

Another disease which seems linked to dietary factors is athero-sclerosis, the build-up of fatty deposits in the arteries. The consumption of animal fats affects the blood cholesterol level, and people with a high cholesterol level seem more prone to coronary artery disease. Cholesterol is a normal constituent of the blood and is present in all foods derived from animals, particularly pork products, offal, butter, egg yolk, cheese. One way of reducing the cholesterol level is to replace animal fats in the diet by fats of plant origin, such as vegetable oils, and by the type of margarine which contains non-cholesterol fats. Not eating foods which themselves contain a lot of cholesterol also helps to control the level in the blood. A report *Fats and your health* was published in *Which?* September 1976.

Exercise

Many men by the time they have reached their fifties find that regular exercise is difficult to obtain. The desk, the motor car, the television set, keep them chairbound for long periods of the day. To make matters worse, food often continues to be indulged in despite the reduced need for it. From the health point of view, disuse of the body is misuse. The body is remarkably flexible and mobile and, when in good trim, capable of an enormous output of energy. Left idle, changes take place which are a threat to health and survival. Muscles that are under-exercised lose strength and bulk, and fat accumulates readily—not only where it is visible around the middle, but also where it has packed in and around internal organs such as the heart, kidneys and intestines.

It is better to take exercise regularly than to go exercise-crazy now and again. Taking up exercise vigorously after a long period of physical inactivity is harmful. So, if you are out of condition, start by walking more—up to an hour a day every day. You can do muscle-tightening exercises in the car, press-ups in the bedroom, some pacing or heel-raising in the office. Walk up stairs instead of using the lift or escalator. When you are fit, you should carry out vigorous exercises for a short period each day—bursts of exercise that will send the pulse racing and produce mild sweat. But do this only when you have gradually worked up to being fit.

Although it may not be advisable to take up a strenuous sport—such as squash—in middle age, you should continue with (or take up) any sport you can do at your own speed such as swimming, golf, tennis, langlauf ski-ing, bicycling. The important thing is not to give up a sport or game because you now have less time and energy for it. Fresh air, the exercise and, for many sports, the company, help to make you feel and function better.

When you are standing or walking, be aware of your posture. Backache is common in middle age. Much back trouble can be prevented if the back and abdominal muscles are kept strong and in good tone and if you avoid stress on the spine, particularly in the region of the lower back. Do not lift with the back bent forwards: try to keep the back straight and use your leg muscles to help lift. Your posture when sitting is important, too. A chair should support the small of your back and allow you to sit tall.

If you feel stiff when you wake in the morning, it may be for no other reason than that the bed is unsuitable. For good support, and a comfortable night's rest, the mattress should be firm and should not give by more than about two inches at any part. If your mattress is beginning to sag, buy a new one.

Sleeping

Sleep has always been something of a mystery, but it is known that the quality of sleep is far more important than its duration. Getting as much sleep as possible is by some people considered a recipe for good health. They can become somewhat fanatical about making sure that they get their sleep, and may even abruptly terminate social engagements in order to get to bed at a certain time. However, sleep is generally more a characteristic of good health than a creator of it.

By middle age, the pattern of sleep is established, some people sleeping generally longer and deeper than others. Sleep can vary in quality: a short deep sleep may be more refreshing than a whole night's restless sleep. There is no rule about the number of hours' sleep a person needs—anyone who wakes up feeling tired has probably not had enough.

Sleep is a habit which, if it is broken for whatever reason, can sometimes be difficult to re-establish. Several things commonly interfere with sleep: an uncomfortable bed, a stuffy or draughty room, feeling too hot or too cold, too much light, too much noise, a restless spouse, hunger or having over-eaten, being over-excited, ill or in pain.

When you cannot sleep, it may be better to read for a while something that is not too demanding or exciting than to lie fretting and bored in the dark. Getting up to have a smoke or a cup of tea can make things worse, because these are stimulants. If the cause is insufficient fresh air and exercise during the day, half an hour's brisk walk in the evening may help.

A *Which?* report on sleep (July 1978) discusses different methods of overcoming sleeplessness.

Insomnia is the persistent inability, real or imagined, to sleep. One type of insomnia is difficulty in falling asleep at bedtime, usually due to some anxiety or nervous tension which keeps the mind from resting. This can set up a vicious circle in which worry leads to lack of sleep and this leads to the further anxiety of whether sleep will come or not. Reliance on sleeping pills is not the solution: getting into the habit of taking sleeping pills may produce a situation in which sleep will not occur naturally so that the condition becomes chronic.

The other type of insomnia is not the problem of failing to fall asleep, but of waking in the very early hours, unable to get to sleep again. Anyone waking up very early feeling fresh, well and ready for a day's work has probably had enough sleep and is not suffering from real insomnia. However, people who repeatedly wake in the early hours and feel tired and depressed require treatment and should consult their doctor.

Alcohol

Many myths have grown up about the value of alcohol, and social rituals lend a glamour to its use. Alcohol is commonly used to promote good fellowship and to break down tension and inhibition. A substance that can overcome social and personal barriers, where they exist, comes to be highly regarded so that other qualities are attributed to it. It is believed by many to be a stimulant, an appetizer, a means of keeping the body warm or 'keeping out the cold'.

Alcohol is very rapidly absorbed and diffused throughout the body, and begins to act on the brain in a matter of about ten minutes. It depresses the nervous system and by its action on the higher brain centres that control behaviour, it reduces perception and restraint on primitive, aggressive and amorous impulses.

Judgment is impaired in proportion to the amount drunk. Driving performance suffers—after only a couple of whiskies one is less aware of danger and over-confident in taking risks, even though feeling oneself to be sharper and more alert for a while.

The 'stimulant' effect of alcohol is created by the sense of release and expansion which accompanies the loosening of inhibitions. One laughs more readily, and becomes more loquacious, revealing more of one's real feelings—hence the saying 'in vino veritas'. There is little harm in this while one is in good company; the harm comes when one tries in solitude to use the magic in the bottle to overcome sadness or inadequacy.

The improvement of appetite by an aperitif is not so much due to its alcohol content, but to the aromatic esters added to it. With beer, it is the bitter taste rather than the alcohol that puts an edge on the appetite.

The sense of warmth experienced after a few drinks is due to the opening up of the blood vessels in the skin, which becomes flushed. Whereas the body normally reacts to cold by shutting down the skin circulation in order to conserve heat, alcohol impairs this mechanism, and heat is steadily lost to the surroundings, so that the body cools down rapidly, sometimes down to dangerous levels. Because of this, people could come to grief after tanking up at the local before walking a mile or two home in the depths of winter.

Like any other drug that makes you feel good, alcohol is potentially addictive. Increasing affluence in middle age for many people makes it easier to drink more alcohol, not just socially and cheerfully but as a form of escapism.

Consumption may increase during periods of stress, and later a form of dependence may develop. To produce the desired effect each time larger amounts need to be taken as the body develops tolerance to it. These larger amounts, taken regularly, cause the health to suffer, particularly if alcohol replaces food.

Drinking strong spirits frequently and in large quantities damages the stomach lining. You can usually feel the passage of a measure of spirits down into the stomach, and you would be alarmed if you could see the colour change that takes place in the stomach lining. It is not so bad when the drink is watered down or food is taken at the same time, which dilutes or absorbs the alcohol. Regular spirit drinking on an empty stomach eventually causes a chronic gastritis.

Chronic overuse of alcohol will damage liver cells and is a common cause of cirrhosis of the liver. Even a single large dose of alcohol can affect the liver of a healthy man for a time. A high intake of alcohol reduces the appetite, so that the diet lacks some of the substances which are important for maintaining the health of the liver. The liver is a very complex organ with many functions and when it begins to go wrong, the effects are widespread. In the treatment of cirrhosis, the first thing is to cut out alcohol.

It is important that abuse of alcohol should be recognized in its earliest stage. If you cannot do without a drink for a whole day, you can consider yourself in danger of having a drinking problem. It should be regarded as an illness, rather than as a social disgrace. Many mild alcoholics show no very obvious features but may be quite handicapped in their work and difficult at home. An early sign may be a form of amnesia about what happened the night before.

A symptom of alcoholism is that food cannot be faced in the morning and may even provoke nausea or vomiting. Weight loss may occur and, as the liver becomes affected, the skin acquires a slightly yellow tinge. Eventually, the alcohol-dependent person suffers bouts of uncontrollable shaking of the hands and arms, coming on especially in the early morning. Emotion is blunted and coarsened, behaviour deteriorates and the strain placed on the family and on the loyalty of friends and colleagues increases. Awareness of these additional stresses may increase consumption.

Alcoholism is a severe progressive illness and requires medical treatment like any other illness. Treatment which can arrest the condition depends on the recognition that alcoholism is a disease and not a moral failure. It is better to seek help than to make half-hearted resolutions which are easily broken; it is difficult to help someone who is not strongly motivated to stop.

Anyone who suspects that he or she, or someone close, is becoming an alcoholic should get help from a doctor or consider consulting the National Council on Alcoholism (3 Grosvenor Crescent, London SW 1X 7EE; there are affiliated regional councils) or Alcoholics Anonymous, an organisation for recovered and recovering alcoholics to help each other by means of group therapy (membership is free and strictly confidential). If no AA group is listed in the local telephone directory, write to Box 514, 11 Redcliffe Gardens, London SW 10 9BG. There are also Al-anon groups for the family and friends of alcoholics (information from 61 Great Dover Street, London SE 1 4YF).

The June 1978 *Which?* report on alcohol discusses the effects of alcohol, how strong different drinks are, how much alcohol is too much, where help can be sought; it includes a drinker's check list to assess whether someone has a drink problem.

Smoking
Cigarette smoking is the greatest health risk that mankind has
ever inflicted on itself. Someone who smokes a packet of cigarettes every day not only runs twenty times the normal risk of
lung cancer but also runs a much greater risk of other killing
diseases, particularly in middle age. The report on *More about
smoking* in the February 1975 *Which?* said that 'About one
smoker in four dies prematurely because of his smoking—usually
from lung cancer, chronic bronchitis, emphysema or coronary
heart disease. Other diseases linked with smoking include cancer
of the mouth, oesophagus, larynx and bladder; hardening of the
arteries in the legs; gastric and duodenal ulcers; gingivitis and
loss of teeth. The more you smoke and the more you inhale, the
greater the risks.'

The burning cigarette allows the lung to take in carbon monoxide
which displaces some of the oxygen that is needed, and the
nicotine temporarily affects the blood pressure. Smoking reduces
physical well-being and athletic performance. Thus, a 20-ciga-
rettes-a-day man is as affected as if he were 1000 metres above
sea level—although he would only notice this if he had to run for
a bus.

The smoker who throws away his cigarette after a few puffs is in
less danger than the man who smokes it right down to the end,
because it is in that end that the harmful substances become
concentrated. Switching to cigarillos is not healthier—in fact, the
danger is increased where people smoke cigarillos in the same
way as they smoked cigarettes. Health-wise, pipe and cigar
smokers are probably better off only because they tend not to
inhale the smoke.

Even if you have smoked for many years, it is still worth stopping because statistics show that the risk of cancer diminishes progressively until after about ten years it is no greater than for non-smokers.

There is no easy method of stopping smoking; no drug has yet been found which consistently helps withdrawal. The smoker who likes to have something in his mouth might try a dummy cigarette. Astringent lozenges which cause a bad taste after smoking help some people. A tranquillizer may be prescribed by the doctor, and there is hypnosis, and aversion therapy. However, the one necessary and essential step is to decide to stop smoking. Most failures are people who have decided only to try to give up smoking rather than having made a firm decision to stop. Once convinced about giving up smoking completely, do not expect to succeed unless you have great willpower.

Many people are grateful for the sore throat or attack of flu which produces a temporary revulsion for smoking. The longer you can stop like this, the more nicotine is removed from the body and the less the craving. If and when you go to light up, stop and think why you have done it. You may then learn something about your reaction to boredom, anger or frustration. A non-smoking wife or husband can be a great help and work colleagues are often more helpful if they know that you are trying to stop. But there is a strange perversity in some people who delight in seeing you fall from your resolve, or who tempt you to begin again. The temptation may be hard to resist at certain times, such as following a meal or when with a certain group or person, but if you can conquer peak moments of intense desire to smoke, you should be well on the way to being able to give it up altogether.

The Health Education Council's leaflets about not smoking are available from 78 New Oxford Street, London WC1A 1AH (send a stamped addressed envelope) and from area health authority offices. The Chest, Heart and Stroke Association issues pamphlets about the effects of smoking and how to stop (single copies free, from Tavistock House North, Tavistock Square, London WC1H 9JE). Action on Smoking and Health (ASH, 27–35 Mortimer Street, London W1N 7RJ) campaigns to discourage smoking and encourages research into the health hazards of smoking; it also distributes leaflets and notices about the harmful consequences of smoking.

Some nicotine ex-addicts are as likely to relapse after a single smoke as are alcoholics after one drink. Once you have managed to give up smoking, never take another cigarette.

Diseases common in middle age

Although previously common causes of death such as tuberculosis, pneumonia, scarlet fever, have been almost defeated, middle age to-day is a dangerous time for men from the point of view of health and a difficult time for women. Since the beginning of the century, all other age groups such as the foetus, the infant, the school child, the expectant mother, the elderly, can expect improved chances of survival; men in the middle years of adult life are the only group where the death rate has not declined in the developed countries.

Although women in this country have a somewhat longer expectation of life than men, there is no cause for complacency so far as they are concerned. Much of the advice given to men applies to women, too.

If you feel unwell or notice that you now need to do things in a markedly different way, do not dismiss such slight symptoms as mere signs of approaching age. Go and see your doctor about any symptom. This may enable him to recognise disease in its early stage, when it is only a tendency rather than actual illness, and to carry out treatment at a time when it can be effective. He can then also check your blood pressure and urine, and send you for specialist examination if necessary, and advise you on what you should do to keep yourself in better health. Many diseases come on insidiously and can be dealt with or avoided if action is taken in time.

Circulatory disorders

After the age of forty-five, cardio-vascular disorders begin to be an increasing problem, particularly coronary artery disease. It seems to be associated with prosperity and calories, stress and heavy smoking, animal fats and inactivity, but no one factor is responsible: it is the penalty to be paid for a whole way of life.

The heart is about the size of a clenched fist, and is situated just to the left of the centre of the chest. In health, it is probably the strongest organ of the body, capable of responding to any demands made upon it. It consists of four chambers, two (called atria) for collecting blood, situated above two more massive and muscular chambers (called ventricles) designed to pump the blood. The right ventricle pumps blood through the lungs and the left pumps blood to the rest of the body. In order to do this, the heart muscle needs a good supply of blood itself, and this is supplied through the coronary arteries. To be able to respond to action, and emotion, by increasing its output, the heart must have ample blood of good quality, supplied through blood vessels capable of delivering this oxygen-rich blood in response to demand.

high blood pressure

A certain level of pressure is necessary within the blood circulation, and higher levels may be required during times of sudden stress. When the stress is over, the pressure falls to normal levels again. Blood pressure maintained at constantly high levels (hypertension) places a permanent strain on the heart.

Permanent raised blood pressure leads to kidney damage and increases the risk of a heart attack or a stroke. The early warning signs of high blood pressure are unnatural tiredness, shortness of breath, getting up at night to pass urine, pain in the chest. However, hypertension does not always cause symptoms and may simply be discovered as the result of a routine medical check-up. Levels of blood pressure are often set by genetic factors. If a good look round the family, particularly at parents and brothers, reveals a coronary attack, a stroke, or other vascular disease, it is worth going to the doctor for a check.

Treatment for high blood pressure will in the first instance be directed towards the person's life style. Someone with an excessive amount of drive and competitive spirit will be advised to delegate some responsibilities, and take more rest and recreation. An overweight person will be told to lose weight. The doctor may recommend cutting down on salt intake. Control of blood pressure levels is a difficult business, involving drug therapy which may require numerous adjustments and regular visits to the doctor before control is satisfactory. Treatment will be suggested by your doctor even if you have no symptoms, to guard against physical deterioration. It is much easier to accept treatment when you have gone to the doctor to seek relief from the symptoms of an illness, but when you have felt nothing to be wrong, you may feel that he is making a fuss. What makes things more difficult is

c

that the treatment must be continued for a number of years. Perseverance is rewarded in the long run by greater reserves of energy and a better expectation of life.

coronary artery disease
The deposition of a porridge-like material beneath the lining of the arteries is called atheroma. A diet high in animal fats, lack of exercise, and smoking, are jointly hazards associated with atheroma deposits. The effect of this obstruction in the arteries is to reduce the blood flow to the organs they supply. The silent infiltration of the coronary artery walls by atheroma proceeds to narrow the artery until the blood flow through it is reduced to a critical level. A warning of this is abnormal tiredness.

—angina pectoris
Where the coronary arteries are narrowed by disease, a critical situation occurs during exercise or emotion when the needs of the heart muscle exceed its supply of blood. When this has happened, a heavy pain of a constricting or gripping character is felt in the middle of the chest just behind the breast bone or as a tight band running around the chest. It may radiate down the left arm, or pass up into the neck, or to the teeth. This is called angina pectoris. Once the sufferer has rested so that the demand has stopped, the pain stops. It recurs after the same amount of exertion; for example, every morning at the same place on the steps leading up to the railway platform. It is more likely to occur after a meal, so people often put this pain down to indigestion. The warning may be ignored because the pain is misunderstood by the man who stops to put an indigestion tablet in his mouth: it is not the tablet but the act of stopping to take it that relieves the pain. It is vital, therefore, to recognize this condition, and report it to the

doctor. The doctor can prescribe tablets to suck or chew which will stop an attack. Angina pectoris can in many cases be brought under control by reduction of weight, a low cholesterol diet, and giving up smoking, plus, if need be, a quieter life altogether.

—coronary thrombosis
It is normal for blood to clot when we cut ourselves, but it is not normal for blood to clot inside the blood vessels. When it does so, it is called thrombosis. Thrombosis will not occur where the surface lining of the blood vessels is smooth and undamaged, but is always a possibility where the artery walls are roughened by deposits of atheroma. These clots are likely to cause complete obstruction where they form, or they may dislodge and be carried away by the bloodstream to form a blockage farther along the artery at a point where it narrows and divides.

The occurrence of thrombosis in a coronary artery is a medical emergency. Pain is felt in the centre of the chest, gripping and agonizing in character, perhaps radiating into the arm or neck. It comes on unpredictably and, unlike the pain of angina pectoris, is not relieved by rest. There should be no delay in summoning a doctor and, until the doctor arrives, the patient should rest without moving, supported in a comfortable semi-reclining position, with a good supply of fresh air. The speed with which he receives medical aid is important. Acute coronary care units have been set up in most district general hospitals for dealing with severe cases.

The emphasis in aftercare is on rehabilitation and the return to as active a life as possible, so as not to become a cardiac invalid. The scar in the heart muscle is often much less significant than in the person's mind. You should co-operate with the doctor in his encouragement of you to lead a sensible life, avoiding peak or prolonged exertion or excesses.

arterial disease in the legs
When blocking of the arteries in the thigh occurs, a tight severe pain is felt in the calf muscle after walking a certain number of paces, preventing the person from walking farther. As with angina, standing still or sitting makes the pain wear off. This condition is called intermittent claudication. The damage to the artery cannot be undone except by complicated surgery, but a better delivery of oxygen in the blood supply helps, so the first thing the doctor will advise a smoker is to give it up immediately.

varicose veins
Prominent and dilated superficial veins on the legs are a common disorder. Apart from the disfigurement caused by varicose veins, they cause the legs to ache and feel heavy, and to tire easily. Varicose veins are made worse by prolonged standing and by being overweight. More serious complications may arise such as varicose ulcers or phlebitis (inflammation of the vein).

Varicose veins develop because of the impaired ability of the veins to return the blood from the legs against the effects of gravity. There are two main reasons: either the valves in the veins which join the superficial system to the deep system are faulty and allow a back-flow which dilates the superficial veins, or the veins themselves dilate because they have weak walls and poor support from the surrounding tissue. Provided that there is no underlying problem in the deep veins, the superficial veins can be effectively treated by surgery or by injection (sclerotherapy).

In minor cases, and where there are no grossly incompetent valves at points which cannot effectively be bandaged, the veins can be treated by injection; this must be followed by the continuous wearing of firm bandages for as long as six weeks. One of the commonest sites of valve failure is in the groin, and this cannot be treated by injection because it is impossible to bandage the upper thigh, and therefore an operation is required to remove the vein. This operation involves only a brief hospital admission—sometimes for just a day. The vein on the back of the çalf requires similar treatment when it is faulty. Within one or two days of the operation, the patient can walk fairly well, and should soon be able to resume an almost normal life. If there is extensive bruising associated with large veins, there may be more discomfort which takes a little longer to settle. At present, there is a long waiting list for NHS treatment for varicose veins; wearing support stockings meanwhile may give some relief.

Respiratory disorders
The common respiratory illnesses in middle age are bronchitis, pneumonia and cancer of the lung. These diseases are more common by far in cigarette smokers than non-smokers, and town dwellers are more affected than country dwellers.

Lung cancer is directly associated with smoking, particularly in an urban area where atmospheric pollution increases the hazard. Early symptoms are a worsening of the smoker's morning cough, pain in the chest, spitting blood. Surgery is the only possible cure; only a small percentage of lung cancer cases can be cured. Giving up smoking, even after years of the habit, can diminish the risk of getting lung cancer. After about ten years of abstinence, there is only a slight difference between the ex-smoker and the non-smoker as far as risk of cancer of the lung is concerned.

bronchitis
Bronchitis has its origins in repeated childhood infections, smoking, air pollution at work and at home, and our climate. Chronic bronchitis is so common in this country that elsewhere it is called 'the english disease'.

Inhaling irritant matter causes an abnormal amount of mucus to be produced in the bronchial tubes as a protective response. The excess mucus coats and clogs the bronchial tubes, obstructs the airflow and allows infections to settle in the membrane lining the tubes, causing inflammation. The membrane is damaged, the excessively thick mucus blocks the air passages, and breathing—both in and out—becomes progressively more difficult, eventually throwing a strain on the heart.

To avoid chest disorders, you must not smoke, should exercise regularly and keep your weight at a sensible level. Stopping smoking always helps. (Smokers often feel no benefit from stopping smoking for three months or so, but even in chronic cases a definite improvement will follow in time.) If you are overweight, get rid of it because abdominal fat prevents the lungs expanding fully.

A bronchitic person should try to avoid closed stuffy rooms where one might catch an infection from someone else. In the winter, and particularly on foggy nights, sleep with the window closed leaving the bedroom door open to allow ventilation. Do not go from a hot fireside into an ice-cold bedroom. If you cannot afford to warm the bedroom, try to warm the bed before you get into it. Winter is a dangerous season for bronchitics, and the time to take particular care of yourself. If you get a chest infection, do not neglect it. If the phlegm turns yellow, coughing increases and breath gets shorter, do not delay in seeing the doctor. Waiting only allows infection to spread and damage or destroy more of the lung tissue.

Digestive disorders
Digestive disorders range from constipation to cancer of the colon and include gastric ulcers, gall bladder disease, diverticulitis. Some are thought to be due to a lack of vegetable fibre in our diet, and that eating a heaped dessertspoonful of unprocessed bran with breakfast every day would help to prevent many digestive disorders. The proof of an unrefined diet is in the eating.

As well as eating suitable foods, one should eat in moderation and calmly. Not only the food you eat but also your state of mind affects the digestive process because, more than any other part of the body, it becomes upset when you are upset.

Smoking, strong alcoholic drinks, and some drugs contribute to digestive disorder. The lining of the stomach, although remarkably tough, can be damaged by various medicines, including aspirin and its derivatives. People often prescribe an aspirin for themselves for minor aches and pains, such as a headache or toothache, but no one should take aspirin regularly except on the doctor's advice.

ulcers
Duodenal ulcers are more common in men than women and generally begin to make their presence felt between the ages of 30 and 40. Ulcers most frequently afflict the tense and perfectionist person, but no one is immune. The cause of ulcers is not known, and therefore it is difficult to suggest how they can be prevented. It seems sensible to avoid rushed meals, at irregular intervals, accompanied by smoking and spirits. Stress, no doubt, plays an important part.

The symptoms are pain in the pit of the stomach, relieved by milk or indigestion tablets, and worse before meals and in the early hours. Symptoms often last for 4 to 6 weeks and then abate for a period of months or years.

The doctor will advise on taking antacids and on an appropriate diet, probably stressing the need to avoid fried and fatty foods. Ulcer pain is often felt at night, and sufferers soon learn to keep a glass of milk by the bed as a means of relief.

Apart from the pain and misery they cause, ulcers can endanger life by their complications, which usually occur suddenly and without warning: for instance, an ulcer may perforate, causing the release of digestive juices and food into the abdominal cavity, resulting in a state of collapse and shock. Or an ulcer may bleed—the blood may be revealed by a dark tarry stool passed some hours later. A small haemorrhage may cause vomiting, in which blood mixed with gastric juice has the appearance of coffee grounds.

When pain is persistent in spite of medical treatment and associated with a lot of vomiting, surgery may be considered.

diverticulitis
A common condition of the lower bowel that occurs over the age of 35, diverticulosis is often associated with obesity and varicose veins. Diverticula are small pouches protruding from the colon, possibly due to a raised pressure within the bowel. If these become inflamed (diverticulitis), they cause pain and discomfort. Until recently, people with diverticulosis were advised to avoid eating the pips and skin of fruit. However, it is now thought that it is the lack of such fibrous residue in the diet that causes this condition, so an unrefined diet high in vegetable fibre—wholemeal bread, fresh fruit and vegetables—is now recommended.

Such a diet also leads to more rapid elimination of harmful breakdown products by shortening the transit time through the bowel.

gall bladder trouble
Inflammation of the gall bladder (cholecystitis) and the formation of gall stones tends to occur in middle age more in women than men. It seems to affect those who are overweight rather than the thin and active, and in some cases is associated with diabetes. The symptoms are dyspepsia, tenderness below the ribs on the right-hand side or pain at the shoulder. In severe cases, there is jaundice. Gall stones can form without causing any symptoms, but if they cause pain or discomfort, or obstruct the flow of bile, the stones may have to be removed by surgery.

Diabetes

Diabetes is a metabolic disorder in which the body's ability to utilise carbohydrate is impaired; the sugar is excreted in the urine and lost to the system. Diabetes in late middle age is sometimes discovered as a result of routine examination of the urine, or because of one of the complications of the disease affecting the eyes, skin or nervous system. It is often difficult to tell, even by tests, whether a person is a diabetic because it is possible for there to be sugar in the urine in completely normal individuals. Sugar may appear in the urine temporarily in the poorly nourished, after an accident, an operation or a stressful illness, in associated with some hormonal disorders, and as a result of taking certain drugs.

Those who develop diabetes under the age of forty usually do so in a dramatic fashion with raging thirst, loss of weight and weakness, frequent and excessive urination as the main symptoms, and so gain early attention. Generally, symptoms are less in the older age group, although increased fatigability and dryness of the mouth may be noticed, and there may be inflammation of the vagina and vulva, or of the foreskin, with intense itching. Diabetes is more prevalent in overweight people.

Treatment may consist of diet alone or of diet plus tablets or of diet plus insulin injections. The prescribed diet may be low in carbohydrate or calorie restricted. Drugs to stimulate insulin-production by the body may be required in those people in whom dieting does not relieve symptoms or lower the blood sugar. The majority of people who get diabetes over the age of fifty do not need to have injections of insulin.

Because of the possibility of complications arising from the condition, a person with diabetes should go to the doctor at regular intervals for reassessment and to ensure that other effects of diabetes are checked. A diabetic person is likely to react adversely to infections and should therefore be as careful as possible not to pick up any infection.

The British Diabetic Association (10 Queen Anne Street, London W1M 0BD) publishes leaflets on the management of the disease, available separately or bound in a stiff cover as *The Diabetic's Handbook* (£2); other publications include *Carbohydrate Countdown* (65p) listing many everyday foods with their carbohydrate and calorie values, and *Successful Diabetic Cookery* (£1.25).

The menopause

Most women think of middle age in terms of the menopause, when they cease menstruating. Menstrual periods usually cease between the ages of 47 and 52, give or take a couple of years either way.

the ovaries

The ovaries are the female sex glands. There are two in the abdominal cavity, each about the shape and size of a small walnut. There is a covering layer of cells and, inside, the numerous follicles which contain the ova (eggs). During a woman's reproductive life, about 400 ova are shed. There is no mechanism for replacing follicles, so eventually all become used up and the reproductive capacity is lost at the menopause.

The control of ovarian function is complex, involving the regulating centre in the brain called the hypothalamus and the pituitary gland attached to it. The link between hypothalamus, pituitary and ovaries is by chemical substances (hormones) secreted into the blood. By means of its hormones, the pituitary gland influences several other endocrine glands, such as the thyroid and adrenals and, directly or indirectly, most bodily functions such as growth, metabolism, the pressure in the blood vessels, as well as the functioning of the reproductive system. Many of the endocrine glands interact and have an effect on each other; if one is not functioning correctly, others can be affected.

The ovaries, apart from producing ova, have the function of producing two types of hormone, the oestrogens and progesterone. During the first half of the menstrual cycle, the ovaries secrete increasing amounts of oestrogen into the bloodstream.

The lining of the uterus (the endometrium) gradually becomes thicker during the cycle. The maximum amount of oestrogen is found at about the thirteenth day of the menstrual cycle, at the time of ovulation when one follicle reaches maturity, ruptures and ejects the ovum through the outer layer of the ovary and, via the fallopian tube, into the uterus. The oestrogen level drops after ovulation, rises again during the second half of the cycle and falls to a low level after menstruation has taken place.

After ovulation, the follicle which contained the ovum changes and produces the hormone progesterone as well as oestrogen. The lining of the uterus continues to develop under the influence of the two hormones. If the ovum is not fertilised while it passes through the fallopian tube, the level of both hormones falls. This causes menstruation, during which the lining of the uterus is shed together with some blood and mucus.

With the onset of a woman's so-called change of life, the whole hormonal picture changes. While the body's other endocrine glands continue to produce their special secretions directly into the bloodstream throughout life, the function of the ovaries is limited in time because of the progressive loss of follicles, and the less effective production of oestrogen. The feedback relationship between ovaries, hypothalamus and pituitary gland changes, with increased activity of the latter two. For a time this may maintain more or less regular menstruation, although ovulation becomes irregular and often ceases before the periods themselves stop. In some women, this phase of altered endocrine relationships leads to prolonged oestrogen secretion which causes excessive development of the uterine lining and this may result in prolonged and heavy bleeding. Later on, follicle activity gradually declines and oestrogen production ceases.

The ovaries atrophy and become smaller, shrinking to the size of an olive. Reduced oestrogen production causes shrinking of the endometrium and muscle, ligaments, and blood vessels of the uterus. The same process takes place in the fallopian tubes and part of the cervix (neck of the womb). The outer genitalia decrease in size and the clitoris also gets smaller. The folds of the vulva and the lining of the vagina become thinner. The breasts become smaller and less firm.

—sex and fertility
These changes take place gradually; the reproductive organs do not wither away at the menopause and it is a fallacy that the menopause means the end of sexual life. The sex drive does lessen in most women, but no woman need lose the capacity for sexual activity nor is it likely to affect her general health adversely. Only occasionally does the loss of the capacity to bear children cause true frigidity. Some woman have their sexual desire heightened for a while and may find themselves masturbating for the first time since adolescence. In cases where the husband is having his own climacteric difficulties—slowing of the sexual drive, diminishing potency and the concern this causes, worries about retirement and other problems—an understanding wife can do a good deal to help them both. Satisfactory sexual intercourse can continue if there is mutual understanding and tolerance between the man and the woman.

After the age of thirty, probably earlier, a woman's fertility begins to decrease, and ovulation may become less frequent. If the menstrual pattern is irregular and the periods become very infrequent, it is difficult to know when ovulation takes place. It may be thought that the menopause has occurred because there has not been a period for a long time; but an ovulation can occur out of the blue and would be followed by a period—unless conception has taken place. It is therefore advisable that some contraceptive measure is used until a year has passed without having a period (two years is safer for a woman under fifty).

Unless a woman has been using the rhythm method as her contraceptive means, there is often no need to consider a change in the method of contraception at or near the menopause. However, difficulty may be experienced in retaining an occlusive cap or diaphragm near the menopause due to some prolapse of the vaginal walls or uterus, and if it is not possible to overcome this difficulty by a change in size of the device, the method will have to be abandoned. The use of an intrauterine device may aggravate bleeding problems in a woman whose periods become very heavy near the menopause.

When a woman on a contraceptive pill continues to take it, she will not know when her menopause occurs. If she stops taking the pill and has periods, she should go back on it for a year or so as a contraceptive measure. Once off the pill, if she has no periods, she has reached the menopause. If she has menopausal symptoms, rather than going back on the pill, which contains more hormones than appropriate for menopausal hormone deficiency, she should seek specific treatment for her symptoms. Some doctors suggest that the contraceptive pill should be discontinued over the age of 45, particularly if the woman is overweight, a heavy cigarette smoker or there is a risk of hypertension.

After the cessation of periods, there may be dryness of the vagina due to the lack of lubrication from glandular secretions. Soreness during intercourse can be overcome by the woman using a water-soluble vaginal jelly, or with the sheath method of contraception by the man using a lubricated condom.

If there is any doubt as to the cause of a missed period, a pregnancy test can be carried out when the period is not less than 14 days overdue. A false positive result may be obtained at or near the menopause because of the large amounts of the gonadotrophic hormone which can appear in the urine. The level of this hormone rises in pregnancy and at the menopause gonadotrophin is produced in large quantities by the pituitary gland because the output is no longer controlled by the hormones from the ovary. If the test is negative, therefore, it means that a woman is not pregnant, but if the test is positive, further confirmation should be sought. A pregnancy test can be carried out under the national health service.

hot flushes

The closedown of the ovaries affects not only ovulation and the hormonal regulation of the lining of the womb, but also has all sorts of other effects, such as changes in the distribution of hair, in the skin and the bones, changes in the sexual urge and in emotional stability. While other glands take over some of the regulating of various body functions, there is usually a time when things become unstable—for instance, the control over the calibre of blood vessels, leading to that uncomfortable hallmark of the menopause, the hot flush.

Hot flushes are the commonest symptom of the menopause and can cause much distress, partly because they are embarrassing and partly due to the odd sensations that accompany them. They are like the adolescent blush in that embarrassment makes them worse but they are not caused by embarrassment and occur independently of it.

The flushes may start before periods ever become irregular, or they may not start until the periods have stopped. Some women never experience them; others are plagued by them, having a dozen or more in the day and then more during the night. Hot flushes can be a cause of insomnia because they can waken a woman from sleep, and she may have difficulty in getting to sleep again.

A hot flush starts with a feeling of physical and mental tension. It is felt first in the chest or abdomen, then a sensation of heat and reddening of the skin spreads from the chest up over the neck and face, and usually over the scalp as well. It is commonly followed by sweating, which relieves the tension. Sweating may be followed by a constriction of the blood vessels which can cause an attack of shivering, and the woman may feel very cold and look pale. The attacks may occur at any hour of the day or night, at shorter or longer intervals. They may last for some seconds or minutes, and may occur several times in one hour or only very occasionally. A flush may spread all over the body, especially at night, with drenching sweat. Such severe flushing may cause exhaustion as well as dread and social embarrassment.

While a woman is experiencing hot flushes, cotton not nylon is best worn next to the skin because of the sweating, and warm clothes should be easily removable. The effect of hot flushes may be reduced by not sitting or standing too close to a source of heat, and by avoiding over-use of coffee, tea, hot or spicey foods, and alcohol. In any case, whatever gives relief should be done.

The cause of flushes is primarily physiological. They stop spontaneously after a while—though sometimes they go on for years. If flushes are troublesome, the general practitioner may prescribe hormone treatment.

the change
At the menopause, the challenge increases to maintain youthfulness, good looks and fitness in order to counteract the natural changes in the body.

A change in shape such as thickening of the waistline occurs even without an increase in weight. This particular deposit of fat is directly due to the loss of the sex hormone. However, this midriff thickening can be kept under control by regular exercises to strengthen the trunk muscles, and attention to diet to counteract the general tendency to put on weight at this time. It is important for menopausal women to make up their minds not to put on weight, not only for their looks but also for their health.

Headaches may occur, particularly of the migraine type, and giddy attacks or dizziness when, although there is a feeling of faintness, the woman does not faint and is relieved merely by sitting down. If these attacks persist for more than a month or two, the doctor should be told. One of the hazards at this age is a rise in blood pressure, and dizziness may occur in a hypertensive person when her rather variable blood pressure is coming down; hypertension can be controlled by treatment. If the cause of the dizziness is ear disease or an infection, that, too, should be treated by a doctor.

Tingling and numbness in the hands and feet, especially at night, may be a result of hormone imbalance, but if it is very troublesome, tell the doctor—it may be a form of neuritis that should be treated.

Fluid retention due to the change in hormone balance, similar to that with which pre-menstrual tension is associated, sometimes causes swelling of the legs and feet. If this is more than transitory, it should be investigated by the doctor in case the cause is chronic vein trouble, or kidney or heart trouble quite unconnected with the menopause.

As a result of changes in the lining of the vagina, some mild inflammation (vaginitis) may occur, resulting in soreness and itching of the vulva, especially at night, discomfort on urinating and pain at intercourse. Bland vaginal jelly or cream that can be bought without prescription may temporarily soothe the symptoms but does not treat the condition. If such a cream does no good, the doctor may prescribe local hormone treatment or oestrogen tablets to be taken by mouth. If local treatment is used, it may be in the form of a cream or pessaries containing oestrogen. The course of treatment usually lasts for a fortnight: one insertion into the vagina at night. There may be some slight soreness in starting this treatment and it is a bit messy.

A thyroid deficiency sometimes occurs at the menopause. This can cause a mental and physical slowing down, a rather bloated appearance, dryness and thinning of the hair, and a tendency to feel the cold intensely. The condition can be reversed by treatment.

General tension may have an effect on the heart, causing a rapid beating with some irregular strong beats or racing of the heart. Someone who becomes aware of a difference in the heart beat may think that she has some heart trouble and be alarmed by it. However, these palpitations are harmless and do not in any way damage the heart. The doctor can reassure you on this and may prescribe a mild sedative to reduce tension. If he should find the palpitations to be due to raised blood pressure or anaemia causing increased output of the heart, he can treat the underlying condition.

Insomnia may arise at the menopause for various reasons. It may be due to hot flushes or to itching of the genitalia or lack of sexual satisfaction, or be part of general nervous tension. It may be a sign of a depressive illness, causing disturbed sleep in the middle third of the night or early waking in the mornings and brooding.

—mood changes
At the menopause, irritability tends to be a problem, and is similar to (and probably has similar biochemical causes as) pre-menstrual tension. Irritability may upset the family peace, especially if there are adolescents or aged parents to deal with who have their own problems. Tension may lead to poor concentration and memory lapses. Or it may make a woman feel that she is going out of her mind. Mood changes include anxiety, depression, crying fits, sometimes aggressive behaviour, apathy or inertia, lethargy, feelings of being inadequate or worthless, occasionally of persecution when she feels that everyone is against her and trivialities may be magnified and lead to brooding and complaints. Less often, prolonged attacks of depression blanket everything, slow a woman down, and make it impossible for her to accept reassurance. These states can be very distressing, they develop insidiously and they may disrupt family life.

Many women feel that they should be able to control these moods by an effort of will, and well-meaning advice of the 'pull yourself together' type is often given. But these moods are not so easily controllable, and in some women lead to increasing exhaustion and depression until a breakdown may become an imminent reality. Although the nervous reactions of this epoch are not heralds of mental disorder, the menopause may precipitate illness in a person who is predisposed to such a disorder.

If, in spite of all efforts, a woman sinks into a depression, it is essential to ask the doctor for some help. There is a particular sort of depressive illness that occurs mainly in older women and was thought to be associated with the end of reproductive life. (It arises often enough during the menopausal years to have been considered the basis of what has been called menopausal madness—one of the most frightening of old wives' tales about the change of life.) The depressive state is marked by unpleasant feelings of worthlessness and guilt, and by the feeling that life is not worth living. People in this state of mind usually have no insight into the fact that they are ill, and need to be persuaded by family or friends to seek medical help. It is important not to disregard any deepening of depression, prolonged lack of interest, loss of former interests, or increase in smoking or drinking habits. Many women suffer in silence, and some become seriously disturbed. This depressive illness can be readily cured, sometimes in a matter of weeks.

A woman who has been a housebound housewife and is now relatively unoccupied at home may find that she has become incapacitated by a dread of being outside the house. This phobia can be a real handicap, making her a prisoner. If it is recognised in time, this condition can be avoided by getting out and about before it ever gets a grip. If it has already become severe or incapacitating, treatment from the doctor may enable a woman to start going out again more and gradually regain her self-confidence. The Open Door Association has been formed to help people who suffer from agoraphobia; send s.a.e. to 447 Pensby Road, Heswall, Merseyside L61 9PQ. If psychiatric treatment is necessary, this may be at a psychiatric day hospital where the woman can go for the day, being taken there perhaps by hospital car or ambulance until she can venture the journey herself.

Another emotional hazard for a woman at this age is an exaggeration of her normal instinct for self-sacrifice—necessary for bringing up children but when the children no longer need continuous and self-effacing attention and care, this instinct can turn into an unpleasant form of martyrdom which makes her own life and the lives of her family impossible. This can be controlled if the woman can realise that she no longer need be self-sacrificing, that her sacrifices of the past are recognised in the form of her grown children and that the time has now come for her and her husband to enjoy their life together. It is, however, not always easy to give up an attitude that one has had for years, particularly when it has in the past been an admirable one.

At this time of life, partly because of the physical and nervous disturbances arising from the menopause, it can become particularly difficult for a woman to respond to challenges and cope with changes in the pattern of life, such as children leaving home, husband having his own troubles or a last fling, the realisation that time is flying. Often, at this time, a woman in the space of a few years sees her children leave home, loses her own parents, watches her husband facing the problems of retirement, and experiences her menopause; it is not surprising that life then appears bleak. One woman may feel that she no longer matters to anyone and that her life has become meaningless, another will make excessive demands on her husband and friends for support, a third will enjoy her newfound freedom and seek new leisure interests. The healthy, happy woman can meet the menopause as just another stage in life. In most cases, readjustment occurs naturally; for others, medical help is needed to overcome moods of prolonged depression. Changes in work and way of life may be helpful, and should be discussed with husband, family and friends. A woman may need to change her job to one of less responsibility rather than give up work altogether, or take sick leave to get over a bad stage.

A woman may have worked herself into a state where a change of environment is essential for the sake of her family as much as herself. Some women benefit from a complete break, such as a holiday on her own or a few days in a retreat. The Association for Promoting Retreats, Church House, Newton Road, London W2 5LS, issues annually a list of retreat houses, in the magazine *Vision* (send 45p). For both men and women at times of great strain and responsibility, retreats can provide an opportunity for a quiet and more detached look at their lives than busy middle-aged people can usually achieve.

Treatment
Fifteen years is a large chunk of a woman's life, during which she may have emotional or physical disturbances unrelated to the menopause and for which she needs specific treatment. Doctors can cause apprehension and resentment when they put down any minor trouble that a woman brings to them anywhere between the ages of 40 and 55 to her 'time of life'. Although many symptoms may be due to hormonal changes, most should be investigated for other causes.

The menopause is not a disease but a normal physiological change. But when menopausal symptoms are troublesome, it is important for someone—it may not always be the woman herself—to realise that treatment is necessary. Symptoms may continue for weeks or months, or even for years, while the woman and her body react to the changes taking place as a result of the ovaries ceasing to produce hormones.

She should not hesitate to express her difficulties to the doctor or her family just because she feels shy, anxious or apathetic—all features of the menopausal state. The doctor may prescribe sedatives to counteract anxiety and irritability or, in some cases, a tranquillizer may be prescribed. There is treatment, including drugs, for depressive illness. Iron can be taken to counteract anaemia. Vaginal itching or pruritis should be investigated and can be treated with specific local applications. Heart symptoms should be reported; they may be due to raised blood pressure which can be treated. The doctor may be able to help with advice on adequate rest, exercise and diet. The family should try to see the situation in perspective and understand the need for tolerance and support.

hormone treatment

Hormone treatment is effective in controlling menopausal symptoms, particularly hot flushes. It usually takes the form of oestrogen, one of the hormones produced by the ovary. The principle behind this treatment is that most, if not all, menopausal symptoms are due to the fact that the ovaries stop producing this hormone in effective amounts; by taking oestrogen, the amount of hormone in the bloodstream is reduced slowly over a period of time while the body adjusts to its change in hormone levels, rather than in an abrupt manner.

Hormone treatment is most usually given in the form of tablets to reduce the extent of hot flushes. The smallest dose which is effective is used and the treatment is given cyclically: in other words, tablets are taken for usually three to four weeks with a one or two week interval between courses. The tablets are generally given for a few months only—three to four on average. This form of treatment is usually gradually tailed off, reducing the dosage rather than stopping abruptly. The main side effect which may be noted from oestrogen treatment is nausea. However, this symptom may be present for only the first few days of treatment and the doctor can adjust the dose or change the type of tablet. Bleeding from the uterus may result from hormone treatment, especially if the dose is too high and treatment is continuous. Any such vaginal bleeding must be reported to the doctor.

In recent years, many specialists have come to suggest that oestrogen should be replaced over a long period, thus cutting out the effect of the menopause entirely. Some practitioners supplement continuous oestrogen therapy with small periodic doses of progesterone which promotes regular bleeding even in a woman past the menopause. Suitably regulated treatment, it is suggested, can reduce the long-term effects of oestrogen deficiency in a woman and counteract some of the effects of ageing and decline. Since there are insufficient factual data to provide conclusive evidence, although the theory sounds excellent, doctors are divided at present on the question of prolonged hormone replacement therapy (HRT). Although there are many theoretical advantages of indefinitely prolonged treatment, it is not yet known what the long-term hazards are.

An increased tendency to blood clots forming (thrombosis) has been noticed in women who have taken oestrogen for a long time. The changes in blood clotting are detected by laboratory tests and there is insufficient evidence whether there is an increase in the number of women suffering from actual clotting disease such as thrombosis in the leg veins, stroke or coronary thrombosis.

The fear that hormone treatment might cause cancer has been raised but there is now some evidence that the use of progesterone with oestrogen in correct doses counteracts any increased tendency to develop uterine cancer.

A degenerative change that starts about the time of the menopause is a thinning of bone (osteoporosis). Bone tissue is not laid down as fast as it is resorbed, leading to increasing brittleness with age. This process seems linked to a decline in oestrogen levels in the blood, and may be arrested although it cannot be reversed through hormone replacement treatment. There is laboratory evidence that osteoporisis may possibly be avoided altogether if treatment is started early enough. However, at least 20 years' clinical followup is required of women starting HRT at the menopause, to know if there is reduced incidence of fractures in old age.

Hormone tablets are available on prescription only, through the general practitioner. At some national health service hospitals in various parts of the country, hormone replacement therapy is offered to suitable patients in menopause clinics or gynaecological departments; there are also a few private clinics. Many women are excluded from HRT because of adverse medical history or the discovery of contra-indications on routine examination. If accepted for HRT, a woman should have regular check-ups and be supervised by her general practitioner or the doctor at the clinic in case any problems develop.

There are at present clinics giving advice or treatment for menopausal symptoms, under the national health service or privately, in Aberdeen, Basingstoke, Belfast, Birmingham, Blackpool, Brighton and Hove, Bristol, Cardiff, Durham, Edinburgh, Glasgow, High Wycombe, Leeds, Liverpool, London, Manchester, Merthyr Tydfil, Mexborough, Mitcham, Newcastle (Staffs), Nottingham, Nuneaton, Oxford, Peterborough, Sheffield, Southport, Stafford, Staines, Stockport, Twickenham, Warrington.

The Family Planning Association (27–35 Mortimer Street, London W1N 7RJ) will send a list of the addresses of NHS and private menopause clinics on request; in some places, there are FPA clinics giving advice on menopause problems.

gynaecological treatment

At the menopause, the periods may stop suddenly. It is more common for the time between periods to become longer and the loss less heavy. If, however, the periods become more frequent, heavier or more prolonged, medical advice should be sought. Frequent floodings may lead to iron deficiency, anaemia and tiredness. Any heavy bleeding or any abnormality in the menstrual discharge should be reported to the doctor. So should bleeding between periods, whether spontaneously or after intercourse.

After the menopause, any bleeding from the vagina should be reported as soon as possible even if it is thought to be a very late period. Usually there is a simple explanation for the symptom, such as a polyp, but it is important to exclude a more serious cause such as cancer. Cancer in the uterus may be completely cured when treated at an early enough stage. That is why a cervical smear is taken as a routine check at most gynaecological clinic examinations; it does not mean that malignancy is suspected.

The general practitioner may refer the woman to a gynaecologist, usually at the outpatient clinic of the local hospital. The interview with the gynaecologist starts with a series of questions about the complaint and past medical history. It is a good idea to have made a note of the date of the last menstrual period. Questions asked about the periods usually include the frequency, duration and the amount of loss. Because women vary in what they regard as a heavy period, the gynaecologist may ask about the number of pads or tampons used, which gives him a rough guide to how heavy the periods are.

An examination includes palpation of the abdomen and the breasts, and an internal (vaginal) examination. The gynaecologist examines the neck of the womb and the walls of the vagina by means of a small instrument called a speculum, and the patient may be asked to cough or bear down. This is to detect any laxness of the walls of the vagina, or any sign of descent or prolapse of the uterus. The uterus and ovaries can be felt by what is known as a bi-manual examination. For this, the doctor places one hand on the lower part of the abdomen and inserts one or two fingers of the other hand in the vagina, so that he can feel the uterus and the ovaries between the two hands.

At some clinics, a routine blood test is made to check for anaemia, particularly if the complaint is of heavy periods.

If the history and examination show anything abnormal, the gynaecologist discusses any further investigations or suggested treatment with the patient. In nearly all cases of unusual bleeding around the menopause or after, a D and C (dilatation and curettage—scraping of the womb) is suggested, this means admission to hospital for two or three days.

—D and C

Dilatation and curettage of the uterus is sometimes carried out simply to establish a diagnosis, but the operation itself may be curative. D and C is carried out under general anaesthesia and the gynaecologist can do a thorough pelvic examination at the same time, while the patient is relaxed under the anaesthesia. The D and C takes only a few minutes. The cervix is gently dilated and a curette, a narrow spoonlike instrument with a sharp edge, is used to remove the lining of the womb in small strips. These are sent to the pathology laboratory for examination. A small piece of the cervix may also be taken for examination if the cervix is inflamed or there is an erosion. Afterwards, the cervix is lightly cauterised with an electric needle. At the curettage, a small polyp in the uterus may be found and removed; it may have been the sole cause of abnormal symptoms.

After a D and C, there is usually slight vaginal bleeding for a few days but there should be no pain. In some women, the first period or two after a D and C is heavier than usual. If the cervix has been cauterised, there will probably be a vaginal discharge for about a month, until the small wound has completely healed.

—fibroids

Fibroids are swellings within the wall of the womb, composed of a form of muscle tissue. If the fibroids are very small, the surgeon may feel them with a curette during a D and C, even if they were not felt by palpation beforehand. The most common symptom they produce is heavy periods because the fibroids enlarge the womb and make a larger area of lining to bleed from. They may also cause symptoms of pressure, such as a heavy feeling in the pelvis or lower abdomen, or a feeling of pressure on the bladder or on the rectum. There is no medical treatment for fibroids; they

D

can only be removed by surgery. However, fibroids do reduce in size at and after the menopause.

The operation to remove fibroids while leaving the womb in place is known as a myomectomy. A cut is made over the fibroid which is shelled out and the wall of the uterus repaired.

—hysterectomy

The operation for removal of the womb is known as hysterectomy.

If a woman has fibroids of a size and a position that they cannot be removed from the womb, the whole of the womb may have to be taken out. That would be a valid reason for a hysterectomy, as would a cancerous growth or pre-cancerous cells indicating the likelihood of a malignant growth. Sometimes even with less obvious a cause it may be suggested that the womb be removed. Although it may be difficult to reply to the doctor's query: 'What do you want your womb for at your age?' if your age is 45, that is not reason enough for having it removed. Hysterectomy is a major gynaecological operation. Before deciding on the operation, a woman should have the opportunity of discussing the matter fully with the gynaecologist and her general practitioner and her family.

The gynaecologist may think he has spent a long time explaining what he is going to do to a patient, and the effects of the operation, but sometimes it is not clear to the woman what is being said because she is tense at the time and takes in only part of the information given. If you are at all doubtful, unclear or undecided, ask for further explanations.

After a hysterectomy, a woman will have no further periods and will not be able to become pregnant. Many women are anxious that if a hysterectomy is carried out, their sex life will be adversely affected. (This often results in delay in seeking advice on gynaecological problems.) Sexual relationship can improve following the operation rather than the reverse: for instance, if previous heavy and frequent periods prevented regular intercourse, or if a woman has had a fear of an unwanted pregnancy. The vagina remains fully functional after a hysterectomy. The top of the vagina does take a few weeks to heal and if intercourse is attempted too early there may be some slight soreness; there is also a discharge which accompanies healing.

Some women are disappointed by the result of the operation. A woman may have been referred to the gynaecologist because of heavy periods, but she may not have stressed her main complaint, which may have been some discomfort or abdominal pain or backache or some farther removed symptoms. She may then have a hysterectomy because it seems indicated for the heavy periods and yet find that she still has discomfort in her abdomen or suffers from backache.

Before an operation, however small, a patient must sign a consent form agreeing to the operation and to the necessary anaesthesia. It is common practice to get the husband to sign the consent form for any operation which renders a woman incapable of bearing children. This does not mean that the operation would not be done without his consent but it prevents him suing the surgeon later. The consent form also says that the patient consents to any further operative measure which may be found necessary during the course of the operation, either in an emergency or if the opened abdomen shows the need for it.

At the operation, the ovaries and the fallopian tubes may or may not be removed. The removal of ovaries is called oophorectomy. Many gynaecologists routinely remove the ovaries when the woman is nearing the menopause; the reason given for doing this is that it is possible that the ovaries may be the site for disease in future years. The question whether to remove the ovaries should be discussed before the operation. But if, at the operation, the ovaries are found to show signs of disease, they will be removed. If only one ovary is removed, there is no menopausal effect. If both ovaries, or a remaining ovary, are removed at the time of the hysterectomy, an immediate menopause is induced. Because surgical removal of the ovaries is abrupt compared with the slow decline in the function of the ovary at a natural menopause, menopausal symptoms are more acute. Hormone replacement treatment can be used to counteract these. If the uterus only is removed, although periods cease, the ovaries continue to function and other symptoms of the menopause do not occur until they would naturally. (A woman who for medical reasons cannot undergo a hysterectomy operation may instead be given radiation treatment to the ovaries and uterus; this generally induces extreme menopausal symptoms.)

A hysterectomy is carried out either through an abdominal incision, or through the vagina. A vaginal hysterectomy leaves no external scar. The uterus can only be removed vaginally if it is of normal size or only moderately enlarged. The operation for vaginal hysterectomy is usually carried out if the patient also complains of some prolapse, because this can be repaired at the same procedure.

—prolapse

Prolapse simply means that the uterus or the vaginal walls have dropped downwards towards the vagina entrance, because of some weakness of the supporting muscles and ligaments which, at the change of life, become weaker and less well developed because of the diminution of hormones. There are many degrees of prolapse and not all give rise to symptoms or require treatment. The majority of women with a prolapse have borne children, but the condition can occur in a woman who has not had a child.

One of the most common complaints is a feeling of discomfort in the vagina, as if a lump were present. If the prolapse is severe, it may feel to the woman as if she noticed something coming down inside, especially towards the evening. There may also be a sensation of discomfort, a dragging feeling in the lower abdomen. Backache can be caused by prolapse and is generally in the middle of the lower back and is quickly relieved by rest, unlike muscular or other back pains.

A prolapse may give rise to urinary symptoms. There may be some difficulty in controlling the bladder, frequency of emptying the bladder or, more rarely, difficulty in completely emptying the bladder; or there may be the symptom of stress incontinence. This last symptom means that the woman leaks a little urine if she coughs, laughs or sneezes, or does anything else to raise pressure within the abdomen. It is not always present with prolapse and does not depend on the amount of prolapse. The urethra (passage from the bladder) in a woman is very short. As part of the defence mechanism to stop leaking when the bladder is full, the urethra joins the bladder at an angle. It is thought that most cases of stress incontinence are caused because this angle becomes altered or lost. Most operations to cure stress incontinence are therefore designed to restore this angle.

If there is only a small degree of prolapse, it may be possible by exercises of the pelvis (similar to postnatal exercises) to remove or delay the need for an operation—but only if the exercises are regularly and efficiently carried out. Another non-surgical method of treatment is to insert into the vagina a supporting ring pessary. A ring pessary will not cure the prolapse but will relieve the symptoms, and a supporting pessary is used sometimes as a test to see whether prolapse is causing the symptoms of which the woman complains—such as backache.

The ring is fitted at the top of the vagina and holds the uterus in a normal, or near normal, position. Fitting is done by a doctor, either by the general practitioner or by a gynaecologist in an outpatient clinic; no anaesthesia is required. It is necessary for a ring pessary to be changed after some months; if the ring becomes hard and dirty, it can cause local infection and inflammation, so it has to be cleaned or a new one inserted. A woman cannot use a diaphragm as a contraceptive device if she has a ring fitted for a prolapse.

If an operation is decided upon, what has to be done varies according to the type and amount of prolapse, and also the patient's age. The repair operation is really plastic surgery to tighten ligaments and muscles and remove excess lining from the vagina. All repair operations are carried out through the vagina and leave no external scar.

One of the after-effects of a repair operation is some soreness or difficulty at intercourse. All repair operations alter the anatomy of the vagina: the vagina is almost always tightened and may also be shortened to some extent. It is important for the surgeon to know whether the woman is likely to want to have intercourse after the operation (the question should always be asked, and answered) since this dictates the type of operation to be performed; it is much easier to construct a short vagina than the long vagina suitable for sexual intercourse.

Following the operation, there may be some small change in the direction of the vagina and the couple will have to adjust to this during intercourse. It is advisable not to leave the resumption of intercourse too long after a repair operation because this may result in some tightening of the entrance to the vagina. Unless otherwise advised, six weeks after operation is an adequate length of time to abstain. If there is any soreness at first due to the tightening or some inflammation of the walls of the vagina, the application of a cream can help and can be prescribed by the doctor. Anyone who has been using a cap or diaphragm as a contraceptive should check at the clinic that the operation has not made it ineffective.

In the majority of cases, a repair operation cures or improves stress incontinence. But if stress incontinence remains, a further vaginal repair may have to be carried out, or an abdominal operation to stitch part of the bladder upwards or support it by a sling.

Elderly dependants

A problem facing many middle-aged women and a comparatively small number of men on their own, is the care of infirm or elderly relatives at home. The task of caring for an old person as well as keeping down a job can quickly result in much isolation: no nights out, no weekends off, no holidays. There are some sources of relief in cash and kind which may help a working woman to keep her job even though she has an elderly person to look after at home.

The financial circumstances of the old person may give entitlement to a state supplementary pension and to various additional benefits. Information can be obtained from leaflet SB1 at post offices and from a local social security office. The household may be eligible for a rebate on the rates or for a rent rebate or rent allowance; the local authority finance or housing department should be asked about these rebates.

Welfare and domiciliary services are provided by the local authority and the area health authority but vary from locality to locality. Many provide day centres for the elderly, nursing care, home helps, meals-on-wheels, good neighbour schemes. Voluntary services of various kinds are run in most places by churches, women's organisations, and other groups. The local citizens advice bureau knows about local groups.

Domestic or nursing help is difficult to come by and may be prohibitively expensive, but even if it means dipping into savings to pay for such help, a woman would be well advised to do so in order to keep on her job as long as she can.

When a woman finds herself compelled to give up her job because the old person needs too much care to be left alone all day, she may be eligible for some financial help from public or private sources. Someone who is not working can claim a state supplementary allowance if income and capital are below a specified level. The local social security office can give information about the latest rules of entitlement.

The poor state of health of the old person may justify a claim for the attendance allowance, paid in addition to any other state benefits, free of tax and without any means test, to someone needing attendance during the day and by night. A lower attendance allowance is paid to those who need attention either during the day or by night. An explanatory leaflet and application form (NI 205) is available from the local social security office. Someone below pension age who cannot work because of having to stay at home to care for a severely disabled relative may qualify for an invalid care allowance. This is a weekly payment which is taxable but is not means-tested. Leaflet NI 212 gives details and includes a claim form.

Voluntary organisations such as the Child Poverty Action Group (1 Macklin Street, London WC2B 5NH) and the National Council for the Single Woman and her Dependants (29 Chilworth Mews, London W2 3RG) can be useful because of their experience in helping women to know what they may be able to get and how to get it.

For someone whose capital, although small, is too large to claim state supplementary benefit, there are various charities which may be able to help with funds or advice, such as Counsel and Care for the Elderly (formerly the Elderly Invalids Fund), the Professional Classes Aid Council, the Royal United Kingdom

Beneficent Association; many charities are listed in the annual *Charities Digest*, available in public libraries. There are also charities which operate only locally or for particular classes of people; some give annuities, some help with the cost of convalescence or recuperative rest.

To those who spend many years caring for the old at home, there comes the difficult time when they are left alone and have to readjust their whole life. This can occur when they themselves are getting on in years and perhaps not in the best of health. Everything should be done to maintain social contacts before this time comes. The National Council for the Single Woman and her Dependants has branches throughout the country, whose members do what they can to help one another.

The spinster who has stayed at home to care for her parents may now feel that her life has been thrown away, but if she can have the courage to accept that she has missed certain elements, she can now look for different outlets and interests.

Psychological aspects of middle age

There are many positive advantages to being middle-aged. For instance, many people are financially better off, which means that they can afford longer holidays and perhaps do things that were not possible or practicable when they were younger. If they are physically fit, they will still hold a relative degree of attraction for the opposite sex and, especially if they are mentally young, they can be helpful and interesting to younger colleagues and friends. Although the pattern of life has generally been set by the forties, people can and do change in middle life, developing new activities, interests and skills, and benefit from an increased self-confidence.

Middle age is a time for revaluation. By the time a man has reached the age of 45, he often feels compelled to take stock of himself and to consider how far he has achieved and fulfilled what was expected of him. In this stock-taking, he may have to face a discrepancy between earlier ambition and present accomplishment. In addition to his wife and children, he may also have responsibilities towards his own ageing parents, or those of his wife. Furthermore, new stresses may be introduced into his working life as economic changes and advancing technology compel him to adapt to altered conditions of work to which younger people react more favourably, and more quickly, threatening his authority. Moreover, his children are growing up and challenging him.

It is a time to face up to who you have become, and to make the most of that person.

Some people are blessed with a balanced temperament and never seem to become ruffled. They are the exceptions. The rest of us have an emotional boiling point which varies with the pressures exerted on us from day to day, and have our various ways of coping and reducing tension so as to prevent mental and emotional strain from taking over.

Emotional tension accentuates characteristics, whether of the pushing individual who always wants to be ahead of others or, at the other extreme, of the person who imagines that he is excluded, slighted or neglected by others. The one who pushes himself forward all the time is in danger of real rejection and the type who imagines himself rejected shrinks away and withdraws into complete isolation. Both should try to get back to a middle course.

The desire always to have your own way is bound to bring you into repeated conflict with others: tension in yourself, and in others, will be lowered if you can learn to give in occasionally—even if you are dead right. Being prepared to make the opening move and learning to cooperate more with others will make personal relationships run more smoothly.

When you give vent to your temper, you feel drained afterwards—and often ashamed and foolish. To rechannel anger and frustration, it would be better to work it off by pitching into some constructive physical activity, such as gardening or polishing or washing the car or clearing out the garage.

Faced with a load of work and pressure, one is tempted to do several things at once. The result is often inefficiency and ineffectiveness. Select the task that most urgently needs your attention, get on with it, and forget the rest. By doing one thing at a time, you may find then that your original estimate of the importance of what needs doing was exaggerated.

The perfectionist often sets himself impossible targets. You will succeed much better by enjoying what you are doing than if you worry about not being able to achieve as much as you think you should. Be sufficiently gentle with yourself to be able to give of your best. Do not expect too much of yourself—nor of others. You are almost certain to feel frustrated or let down if you expect other people to reach the standards you set for them. Your children, friends and colleagues are entitled to develop their own values, with their own virtues and shortcomings.

A well-adjusted life depends on good relationships and involvement in the community so that one grows older without isolation. Trying to discover what is going on, talking to as many different types of people as possible, is often a good way of discovering one's own particular gifts and value. When you are worried, you become preoccupied with yourself. By making the effort of trying to help someone else with a problem, your own worries will be put aside for a while and may then seem less pressing.

Talking in confidence to someone you can trust, and who is interested but not directly involved in your problems, is a help towards clarifying your thoughts, so that you may be able to see a solution. A close relative may be too emotionally involved, and for this reason, too, husbands and wives cannot always help each other. It is not advice that one seeks from the other person so much as the opportunity to ventilate thoughts and feelings that have been pent up.

Middle age is often a period when a man reaches a position of responsibility, bringing more and more anxieties to the conscientious type of individual. The switch on/off mechanism (work/play) may then become faulty. Watch out that you do not structure your life in a way that makes it impossible for you to take a proper holiday. Apart from that, set aside definite times for relaxation and recreation. All work and no play not only makes a dull boy but breeds trouble, particularly for the middle-aged. Find time for recreation in some sport or hobby that you really enjoy, and make a positive effort to forget your work and difficulties while you are engaged in it. This should help you regain drive and enthusiasm for your responsibilities.

The Pre-Retirement Association is a nationwide body concerned with helping people prepare for retirement. Details of its services are available from 19 Undine Street, London SW17 8PP (send 30p postage).

The value and importance of physical fitness to cope with the strains of middle age are considerable. The sense of worth of many men is closely bound up with their athletic prowess, physical capacity and virility. For different reasons, men are as vulnerable as women to the threat of physical decline, or actual illness.

depression
Commons signs of stress and anxiety are difficulty in concentrating, irritability, impatience, getting tired more easily, headaches, backache, trembling, sweating, insomnia. Anxiety is usually accompanied by some degree of depression.

Even though depression is a common major illness of middle age, it is often concealed and not always easy to recognise. A friend or relative may have to take the initiative of getting help from the doctor, since the depressed individual may feel himself unworthy of help or be too lethargic to seek it. It is important that someone suffering from depression should have medical treatment without delay. It is not only useless but also cruel to tell such a sufferer to pull himself together. Symptoms pointing to depressive illness include sleep disturbance, feelings of hopelessness, helplessness, loss of interest in surroundings, and social withdrawal. When identified, such depression can be treated successfully with drugs or by other methods.

The onset of severe depression can be quite sudden and to others appear out of proportion in its severity to the set of circumstances from which it seems to arise. The depressed individual may be tormented with guilt and self-blame, and cannot be persuaded otherwise. Social events and cheerful company have no effect on gloomy self-accusations and slowness of thought. He or she sleeps fitfully and wakes early to brood, and since depression is worse in the mornings, it is then that suicidal thoughts are likely to be acted upon. The need for psychiatric advice should be quickly recognised. Depression of this type can arise in a personality previously regarded as stable. Other people who have not effectively faced their problems earlier in life may become depressed without showing such clear-cut symptoms. The lowering of mood can form a recurring pattern, related to events such as disagreement with colleagues, financial loss, bereavement.

sex and impotence

A man who has had difficulties in adapting to the stressful periods of puberty, adolescence, marriage, parenthood, and who has been unable to deal successfully with anxieties and guilt, is predisposed to go through a psychologically disturbing period with perhaps sexual difficulties in middle age. He may entertain feelings of jealousy in respect of his sons or become over-concerned in the protection of his daughters, reaching a pitch of emotion in which unconscious incestuous overtones may be detectable. He may fail to understand the significance of his wife's reaction to the menopause. He may become increasingly isolated from the family, devoting himself exclusively to his work.

Depression, related to the environment or arising from within the individual, can also disturb sexual behaviour. Loss of libido (sexual drive) is symptomatic of a certain type of depression, and may respond well to its treatment.

Hormonal changes in men occur in a less well-defined way than in a woman. In general, the hormonal changes in ageing men are gradual, often almost imperceptible. It is in a small minority that there are more definite falls in male hormone levels, bearing some resemblance to the comparable climacteric changes in the female.

Generally, the deterioration in sexual performance which some men experience around the age of 50 is not related to hormonal changes. The sex urge inevitably decreases with advancing years; the rate of its decline varies considerably from person to person. Some quantitative changes (less frequent sexual activity) as well as qualitative ones must be expected. Men complain of having lost the sexual urge, or of impotence, or of premature ejaculation, or of recurrent poor erection that prevents successful sexual performance.

It is unusual for a middle-aged man to change his pattern of sexual behaviour suddenly or to a great extent. Hypersexuality—an increased sexual urge directing itself on the spouse or other partners—is rarely a new element in this age group, nor is homosexuality or sexual perversion.

A sudden change of pattern in the sexual behaviour of a middle-aged man may be a sign of trouble. Causes of sexual ill-adjustment include physical illness, toxic factors, psychological factors. Some organic illnesses of the brain have the effect of lifting inhibitions so that latent tendencies, thoughts, ideas come to light, and behaviour may become out of keeping with the normal pattern for the individual. Also, in a depressive illness, a schizophrenic illness, or even a very severe stress of an environmental nature, profound changes in function and behaviour can occur.

Certain physical illnesses decrease sexual performance: for example, diabetes, thyroid dysfunction, diseases of the spinal chord or of the genito-urinary tract. Once the illness is diagnosed and successfully treated, sexual performance is likely to return.

Impotence can occur as a result of misconceptions concerning physical illnesses. A person who has had a heart attack is told by the medical practitioner (and this is reinforced probably by the family) that he must not exert himself. It is then wrongly assumed by the individual that sexual intercourse which appears strenuous should either be discontinued or take place infrequently. Wrong conditioning habits are quickly established if intercourse does not take place, or fails. Loss of confidence follows, giving rise in its turn to a level of anxiety that may be high enough to interfere with normal sexual reflexes. Fear of the illness recurring, added to loss of confidence, brings further anxiety, creating a vicious circle.

If a physical illness is affecting behaviour, the problem can sometimes be resolved through discussion with a medical practitioner or with someone who has had similar problems. A man suffering from an arthritic condition, for instance, may need to take a painkiller half an hour before intercourse is contemplated. Alternative positions or techniques of intercourse may help overcome other problems.

Contrary to common belief, it is doubtful whether there are any drugs capable of heightening sexual urge or improving sexual performance. In most cases, suggestion rather than direct pharmaceutical action is likely to be the explanation for any improved performance. Only in a very few cases does hormone treatment with testosterone preparations given with the aim of general rejuvenation have an effect on impotence. It is likely to have beneficial effects only where there is a deficiency of male hormone, as shown by direct measurement in the blood.

Taking tranquillisers, sedatives or sleeping tablets, either alone or in combination, is likely to decrease sexual urge or performance, as do drugs prescribed for hypertension. Other medicaments, such as some of the ones used in treating gastric or duodenal ulcers, containing atropine or alkaloids of the belladonna group (anticholinergic drugs), may give rise to impotence for as long as the drug is taken. Stopping taking the drug will bring a return to normal sexual function. A man who does not know about the possibility of temporary drug-induced impotence is likely to blame lack of his own masculinity—or his wife—with consequent depression and loss of confidence, or marital tensions, which in turn may cause sexual disharmony.

Alcohol has a depressive effect on sexual function if taken in excess or if indulged in over a long period. In chronic alcoholism, sexual performance is often diminished.

Sexual difficulties can be due to psychological factors such as anxiety, depression or guilt. Anxieties arising from one's work, increased responsibilities, the relationship with the spouse, physical illness or the illness of a close relative—in fact, anxieties arising from any source, whether acute or chronic, play a significant role and can, in vulnerable individuals, give rise to impotence.

Abnormal anxieties, feelings of guilt or depression of one sort or another can disturb the sequence of conditioned reflexes necessary to perform the sexual act, resulting in symptoms of impotence. Awareness of the situation is helpful in reducing some of the anxieties, and the fear of being a failure sexually. Bringing about a change in circumstances where possible is called for, as well as an increased degree of self-awareness. By self-analysis or discussion, problems can be identified and acknowledged, which should help to decrease the anxiety and allow a return to normal sexual activity. Often, it is not overwork as such which causes impotence but the anxiety which initially has led the man to overwork. In such a case, some change in routine is essential and the switch on/off mechanism between work and relaxation may have to be readjusted—if necessary with medical help.

Depressive illness, whether linked to middle age or not, is a cause of impotence. One result of treating the illness is recovery from impotence. Depression linked to external depressing events, such as the death of a relative, which persists beyond the normal adaptive period also can induce sexual ill-adjustment. The remedy lies in taking active steps to adapt to the new situation.

Any action or thought which is likely to arouse guilt is often less well tolerated in middle age when the personality has become somewhat rigid. In an introverted and passive person, impotence can be related to guilt, especially if the spouse has a forceful and overbearing personality, and the man feels guilty because of his inability to reach high standards. Guilt arising from an extra-marital relationship can produce impotence in the marital setting.

Sometimes an infidelity can be revealed as resulting from a long-term poor relationship with the spouse, which has been largely obscured by the presence of the children who have now departed from the parental home. A middle-aged couple may have failed to communicate emotionally for many years but the presence of their children allowed a sort of relationship. Impotence may reflect an unsatisfactory overall relationship between partners, in which the woman must not reject her share of responsibility.

Continued sexual activity is always a sign of health in the partners. Sexual behaviour may need to be adjusted to the physiological changes. Erection may come more slowly and ejaculation of seminal fluid be reduced, or sometimes absent. Some waning of drive in a man often causes panic which itself inhibits erection at intercourse or causes rapid flaccidity of the penis when penetration is attempted. Both partners must realise that the ability of the penis to erect is not lost with age, but it is not a feat that can be performed at will. Slow erection can be helped by the woman's stroking and fondling the penis in a way that gives most pleasure. She can then direct by hand the insertion. Some men find that discharge of semen takes place too soon, even before insertion. Again, the woman can help to delay premature ejaculation by pressing the crown of the penis with fingers and thumb, helped, if necessary, by the man's guiding hand.

Couples who have not experimented with different positions and techniques since their early days may now find some alternatives helpful. For example, if a greater control by the woman is needed, either because the man discharges too soon or because she takes longer to get satisfaction, a position with the woman uppermost or the man seated and the woman facing him astride his lap could be tried. There are many, many ways—whatever pleases both is right. The giving and getting of pleasure and the expression of affection through sexual intercourse should be cultivated well past middle age.

INDEX

INDEX

adapting, 1 *et seq*
ageing, 3 *et seq*, 28 *et seq*
 – physical changes, 3, 6, 10, 23, 25, 28, 57, 72
 – at the menopause, 73 *et seq*, 87
 – and sex, 107 *et seq*
agoraphobia, 82
Al-anon groups, 53
alcohol, 50 *et seq*, 67, 78, 110
 see also drinking
Alcoholics Anonymous, 53
alopecia *see* baldness
anaemia, 23, 80, 85, 90
angina pectoris, 60, 61
anxiety, 49, 81, 85, 107, 108, 110
arteries, disease of, 44, 45, 54, 58, 60 *et seq*
apathy, 81, 82, 85, 106
arthritis, 28, 109
ASH, 56
Association for Promoting Retreats, 84
atheroma, 60, 61
atherosclerosis, 45
attendance allowance, 100

backache, 47, 94, 96, 97, 106
baldness, 3, 15
behaviour, changes in, 52, 81 *et seq*, 102 *et seq*
 – sexual, 107 *et seq*
bifocals, 4
bladder, 91, 96, 98
bleaching hair, 11, 12, 13
bleeding
 – menstrual 73, 86, 89, 90, 91, 93
 – vagina 86, 91, 94

blood pressure, 54, 57, 58, 59, 60
bones, changes in, 77, 87
British Diabetic Association, 71
bronchitis, 54, 65, 66
bunion joint, 25, 26

calories, 33 *et seq*, 58, 70
 – values, 35 *et seq*, 71
cancer
 – of bowel, 44, 67
 – and hair dyes, 14
 – and hormone therapy, 87
 – of lung, 54, 55, 65
 – of uterus, 87, 89, 93
carbohydrates, 33, 34, 42
 – and diabetes, 70, 71
cervix, 74, 89, 91
change of life, 1, 28, 73, 74, 79 *et seq*, 101, 102 *et seq*
 – and moods, 81 *et seq*
 see also ageing, menopause, psychological aspects
charities, 100, 101
Chest, Heart and Stroke Association, 56
Child Poverty Action Group, 100
children, relationship with, 1, 81, 83, 102, 104, 107, 111
chiropodist, 25, 27
cholesterol, 45, 61
circulatory disorders, 58 *et seq*
cirrhosis, 52
claudication, intermittent, 62
climacteric, 74, 107
 see also change of life, menopause
colourants, hair, 11, 12 *et seq*

contraception, 75, 97, 98
corns and callosities, 25.
coronary artery, 58
– disease, 44, 45, 54, 58, 60 *et seq*
– and thrombosis, 61, 87

D and C, 91
dentist, 7, 8, 9
dentures, 6, 9
dependants, 99 *et seq*
depilatories, 16
depression, 42, 49, 81, 82, 83, 106
– and impotence, 107, 108
diabetes, 28, 44, 69, 70, 71, 108
diet, 34, 42, 52, 79, 85
– and diseases, 44 *et seq,* 58, 60, 67, 68, 69, 70
   see also food, weight
digestive disorders, 6, 46, 67 *et seq*
dilatation and curettage, 91
diseases, 57 *et seq*
– and arteries, 60 *et seq*
– and diet, 44 *et seq,* 58, 60, 66 *et seq*
– eye, 5
– heart, 26, 28, 60 *et seq,* 80, 85
– kidney, 26, 80
– respiratory, 65 *et seq*
– and smoking, 54 *et seq*
diverticulitis, 44, 67, 68
dizziness, 79
doctor
– consulting, 5, 15, 22, 26, 27, 53, 57, 59, 66, 79 *et seq,* 85, 89, 109
– treating depression, 49, 82, 85, 106
– and gynaecological trouble, 89 *et seq*

– and hormone replacement, 78, 86 *et seq*
– treatment by, 42, 52, 55, 59, 61, 62, 66, 68, 70, 78, 79, 80, 82, 85, 86, 97, 98
drinking, 28, 32, 33, 82
   see also alcohol
drugs, 67, 85
– appetite suppressant, 42
– aspirin, 67
– and depression, 106
– and diabetes, 70
– and high blood pressure, 59
– sedatives, 28, 80, 85
– and sex, 109
– sleeping pills, 49
– and smoking, 55
– tranquillizers, 55, 85

electrolysis, 16, 17
endometrium, 73, 74
energy, 1, 43, 46
– and calories, 33 *et seq*
– requirements, 29, 31 *et seq*
exercise, 31, 32, 46, 47, 66, 79, 85, 97
– lack of, 28, 29, 46, 58, 60
eyes, 3 *et seq,* 70

face lift, 21, 22
face masks, 19
Family Planning Association, 88
feet. 25 *et seq,* 79
fertility, 74 *et seq*
fibre, vegetable, 44, 67, 68
fibroids, 91, 92, 93
fitness, 1, 28 *et seq,* 54, 57, 79, 105

flushes, hot, 77, 78, 81, 86
follicle
– hair, 10 *et seq*
– ovarian, 72, 73
food, 28 *et seq*, 44, 45, 46, 58, 60
– and alcohol, 51, 52
– and calories, 35 *et seq*
– and digestion, 67 *et seq*
– and teeth, 6, 7

gall bladder, 44, 67, 69
gallstones, 28, 69
gingivitis, 7, 54
glands, 72 *et seq*, 77
– thyroid, 72, 80
glaucoma, 5
gums, 7, 8
gynaecological treatment, 89 *et seq*

hair, 3, 10 *et seq*, 77
– unwanted, 16, 17
   see also baldness
headaches, 4, 67, 79, 106
health, aspects of, 28 *et seq*
   see also ageing, fitness
heart, 46, 58, 59, 65
– palpitations, 80
– trouble, 26, 28, 60 *et seq*, 79, 85
heels, painful, 26, 27
high blood pressure, 28, 59 *et seq*,
   79, 80, 85
   see also hypertension
hormones, 72 *et seq*
– changes in, 16, 72, 73 *et seq*, 79,
   85, 95, 107, 109
– and menstruation, 41, 72, 73

– treatment with 19, 26, 75, 79, 86 *et
   seq*, 95, 109
   see also oestrogen, progesterone,
   testosterone
HRT, 87, 88
hyperkeratosis, 26
hypertension, 59, 75, 79, 109
   see also high blood pressure
hysterectomy, 93 *et seq*

impotence, 74, 107 *et seq*
incontinence, stress, 96, 98
insomnia, 48, 49, 77, 81, 106
intercourse *see* sex, vagina
invalid care allowance, 100
irritability, 81, 85, 106

keratin, 10
kidneys, 41, 46, 59
– disease of, 26, 80
kilocalories, 33

memory lapses, 52, 81
menopause, 72 *et seq*
– and contraception, 75
– and gynaecological trouble, 89 *et
   seq*
– and hot flushes, 77 *et seq*
– and hyperkeratosis, 26
– and physical changes, 16, 73 *et
   seq*, 79 *et seq*
– and weight, 29, 79
menopause clinics, 88
menstruation, 41, 72, 73, 89, 91, 93
mood changes, 81 *et seq*, 106
myomectomy, 92

nails, 23
National Council on Alcoholism, 53
National Council for the Single Woman and her Dependants, 100, 101
national health service
– and eye testing, 3
– and pregnancy test, 76
– treatment, 7, 8, 20, 88

obesity, 26, 44, 68
  see also weight
oedema, 26, 79
oestrogen
– and menstruation, 41, 72, 73
– reduction in, 73, 86, 87
– treatment with, 19, 75, 79, 86 *et seq*
  see also hormones
oophorectomy, 94
Open Door Association, 82
operations *see* surgery
osteoarthrosis, 25
osteoporosis, 87
ovaries, 71 *et seq*, 85, 86, 90
– removal of, 94, 95
ovulation, 72, 73, 74

palpitations, 80
parents, care of, 1, 81, 83, 99 *et seq*. 102
periods, menstrual, *see* menstruation
pill, contraceptive, 75
polyp, 89, 91
pregnancy, 93, 94
– test, 76
Pre-Retirement Association, 105

presbyopia, 3, 4
progesterone, 41, 72, 86, 87, 88
prolapse, 90, 96 *et seq*
proteins
– in food, 33, 34, 42
– and hair, 10, 11, 16
pruritis, 85
psychological aspects, 102 *et seq*

rate rebate, 99
relaxation, 84, 104, 105, 110
rent allowance, rebate, 99
respiratory disorders, 54, 65 *et seq*
retirement, 74, 83, 105
retreats, 84

sebaceous gland, 10, 11, 18, 20
sedatives, 28, 80, 85, 109
sex, 111, 112
– and fertility, 74 *et seq*
– and impotence, 74, 107 *et seq*
– and the menopause, 74, 75, 81
– after an operation, 93, 97, 98
  see also contraception
shoes, 25, 26, 27
skin, 10, 18 *et seq*, 26, 70, 77, 78
– dry, 10, 11, 19, 20
– and hair, 10 *et seq*
sleeping, 42, 48 *et seq*, 81, 106
– pills, 49, 109
slimming *see* weight
smoking, 28, 54 *et seq*, 75, 82
– and diseases, 58, 60, 62, 65, 66, 67
– stopping, 55, 56, 61, 62, 66
stress, 28, 51, 58, 67, 102 *et seq*, 108
stroke, 59, 87
sugar, 6, 34, 42, 44, 70

supplementary benefit, 99, 100
surgery, 21, 22, 26, 28, 62, 63, 65, 68, 69
– gynaecological, 91 *et seq*
sweating, 77, 78, 106
swelling *see* oedema
symptoms, 57, 79 *et seq,* 85
– of alcoholism, 52, 53
– of artery disease, 60 *et seq*
– of depression, 49, 81 *et seq,* 106, 108
– of diabetes, 70
– of gall bladder trouble, 69
– of gynaecological trouble, 89 *et seq*
– of high blood pressure, 59, 79, 80, 85
– of lung cancer, 65
– and the menopause, 74 *et seq,* 85, 86, 95
– of prolapse, 96, 97
– of ulcers, 67

teeth, 6 *et seq,* 54
tension, 49, 50, 77, 80, 81, 83, 103, 110
testosterone, 109
thrombosis, 61, 87
thyroid *see* glands
tranquillizers, 55, 85, 109
treatment, 57, 85 *et seq*
– for alcoholism, 52, 53
– for angina, 61
– for coronary thrombosis, 62, 63
– for depressive illness, 82, 85, 106
– for diabetes, 70
– gynaecological, 89 *et seq*

– for high blood pressure, 59, 60, 79, 80, 85, 109
– with hormones, 19, 26, 78, 80, 86 *et seq,* 95, 109
– for menopausal symptoms, 78, 79 *et seq,* 85 *et seq*
– psychiatric, 82, 106
– for vaginitis, 80, 85
– for varicose veins, 63

ulcers, 44, 54, 63, 68, 109
uterus, 73, 74, 75, 90
– and cancer, 87, 89, 93
– D and C, 90, 91
– and fibroids, 91, 92, 93
– prolapse of, 96 *et seq*
– removal of, 93 *et seq*

vagina, 74, 75, 80, 86, 89, 90, 96, 97
– and intercourse, 76, 80, 94, 98, 99
– and operations, 94, 95, 97, 98
vaginitis, 80, 85
varicose veins, 26, 63, 68
vulva, 70, 74, 80

water
– in the body, 41, 42, 79
– in food, 33, 35
– and the skin, 18, 19, 20
weight, 28 *et seq,* 66
– being over, 25, 26, 28 *et seq,* 46, 58, 59, 63, 68, 69, 75, 79
– losing, 33 *et seq,* 59, 61, 70
– and the menopause, 29, 79
– table of, 30

Which?
– on fats, 45
– on hair dyes, 14
– on moisturisers, 20
– on shampoos, 11
– on sleep, 48

– on smoking, 54
– *way to slim,* 31, 40
womb *see* endometrium, uterus
wrinkles, 10, 18, 19, 21

zest, 1 *et seq*

CONSUMER PUBLICATIONS

Avoiding back trouble
deals with causes of back trouble and gives hints on general care
of the back when sitting, standing, lifting, carrying, doing house-
work, driving, gardening. For those who suffer from back trouble
already, it explains about specialist examination and treatment,
and advises on how to cope with an acute attack.

Treatment and care in mental illness
describes the illnesses concerned and the medical and psychological treatment given on the NHS and privately, and the help
available from the local authority and voluntary organisations.

Having an operation
describes the procedure on admission to hospital: ward routine,
the personnel, preparation for the operation, anaesthesia, post-
operative treatment, convalescence. Basic information is given
about some common operations.

Where to live after retirement
gives detailed information on the pros and cons of housing
alternatives, and the financial aspects involved.

On getting divorced
starts with an explanation of the grounds for divorce in England
or Wales and explains the procedure for an undefended divorce
without a court hearing. The book goes on to deal in detail with
the practical arrangements that have to be made—about the
home, the children, finances—and how problems may be settled.

Health for old age

sets out in lay terms what can go wrong with various parts of the body with increasing age, the physical changes that occur and the treatments available to relieve them.

What to do when someone dies

deals with the procedures that have to be followed after a death: getting the doctor's certificate, registering the death, obtaining death certificates, reporting a death to the coroner and what this entails, arranging for burial or cremation and the funeral. A final section covers the national insurance benefits to be claimed.

Wills and probate

is about wills and how to make one, and about the administration of an estate by executors without the help of a solicitor, with examples. One section deals with intestacy and the difficulties that may arise.

Extending your house

describes what is involved in having an extension built on to a house or bungalow, explaining what has to be done, when and by whom, and how to apply for planning permission and Building Regulations approval.

Central heating

gives the information needed for choosing a central heating system, giving details of the equipment involved, the merits of the different fuels, the insulation required, and discusses finding an installer, having the work carried out, and problems that may arise afterwards.

Which? way to slim
provides sensible advice and information for the would-be slimmer, sorting out fact from fallacy and appraising every aspect of
the slimming problem. It discusses suitable weight ranges, target
weights, the different methods of dieting, exercise, slimming clubs
and aids. The book highlights the danger of being overweight,
particularly the risk of specific circumstances—in middle age,
during pregnancy, when giving up smoking. It includes weight
tables, calorie and carbohydrate charts, recipes and menus, food
values, and gives encouraging advice about how to stay slim.

other **Consumer Publications** include:

How to sue in the county court
An ABC of motoring law
Pregnancy month by month
The newborn baby
Claiming on house, car and holiday insurance
The legal side of buying a house

and in preparation:
Cutting your cost of living

Consumer Publications are available from Consumers' Association, Caxton Hill, Hertford SG13 7LZ and from booksellers.